MW00906026

Running Scared

Running Scared

The Call to Pilgrimage

Thomas D. Maddix

NOVALIS

© 2005 Novalis, Saint Paul University, Ottawa, Canada

Cover design: Audrey Wells
Cover photograph: Lauretta Santarossa
Layout: Caroline Galhidi

Business Office:
Novalis
49 Front Street East, 2nd Floor
Toronto, Ontario, Canada
M5E 1B3

Phone: 1-800-387-7164
Fax: 1-800-204-4140
E-mail: cservice@novalis-inc.com
www.novalis.ca

Library and Archives Canada Cataloguing in Publication

Maddix, Thomas D.
    Running scared : the call to pilgrimage / Thomas D. Maddix.

Includes bibliographical references.
ISBN 2-89507-595-6

    1. Christian pilgrims and pilgrimages. 2. Spiritual biography.
3. Maddix, Thomas D., 1946– –Travel. I. Title.

BL619.P5M32 2005   263'.041   C2005-904689-9

Printed in Canada.

All rights reserved. No part of this publication may be reproduced, stored in a retrieval system, or transmitted in any form, or by any means, electronic, mechanical, photocopying, recording, or otherwise, without the written permission of the publisher.

We acknowledge the financial support of the Government of Canada through the Book Publishing Industry Development Program (BPIDP) for our publishing activities.

5   4   3   2   1   09   08   07   06   05

Contents

Prologue 11

1. The Call to Pilgrimage:
   Life "Between Dreams" 19

2. Pilgrimage: The Ins and Outs 35

3. Chance Encounters 45

4. Touching the Heights and Depths:
   Everest and the Spiritual Journey –
   A Conversation with David Rodney 69

5. Nudges of the Spirit 81

6. Parasites and Spirituality:
   A Sabbatical Journey to Bangladesh.............. 101

7. Breaking Through the Numbness:
   Journal Entries Along the Way 113

8. Sacred Places.. 127

9. Life Lessons 145

Epilogue 163

Notes... 167

Further Reading... 169

Dedication

This book is dedicated to my late mother,
M. Louise Powers Maddix,
who always wondered what I was doing
as I roamed the world,
and to Joan Neehall,
for her persistent encouragement,
questions, direction and support.

What God does first, best and most is to trust people with their moment in history.

God trusts us to do what must be done for the sake of the whole community.

—Walter Brueggemann

Prologue

A note on St. Sarapion the Sindonite, a desert father, fourth century, Egypt:
He travelled once on pilgrimage, to Rome. Here he was told of a celebrated recluse, a woman who lived always in one small room, never going out. Skeptical about her way of life – for he was himself a great wanderer – Sarapion called on her and asked: "Why are you sitting here?" To this she replied: "I am not sitting. I am on a journey."

—Fr. Kallistos Ware, *The Orthodox Way*

My first trip to Europe was in 1973. A colleague and I, teachers at a private school in Ohio, accompanied fifteen high school students on a seven-week, almost first-class tour of European cities. It was a great experience. We started in London and finished in Lisbon, with stops in such cities as Paris, Berne, Salzburg, Venice, Rome and Madrid. But the trip did more than open my eyes to the history and culture of Europe. It made me aware of the power of religious symbolism to capture the imagination and evoke a heartfelt response.

In our travels, we visited countless historic sites, including many churches. Typical of teenagers, the students we accompanied would often moan, "Not another church!" Yet, when we reached Assisi, Italy, and visited the tomb of Francis of Assisi, they paused and reflected. Some were visibly moved. When the tour bus was ready to head out, we had to go back into the church and to the tomb to get some of the students. The power and energy surrounding the tomb were like a magnet for many of them – they did not want to leave. It was there I realized the power of sacred places to make us stop, reflect, go deeper. While no other stop on our European trip had the same impact on the students or on me, something had opened within me, and that something demanded a response. I had the bug. I wanted to explore more.

It was many years before I ventured across the Atlantic again. By this time, my focus had changed. I had done my "familiarization tour," as travel agents call it, with the students, and I was ready for something more profound.

On this second trip to Europe, with my new passport in hand, I didn't head for the usual tourist destinations. Instead, I found my way to the remote village of Taizé, France, the ecumenical community led by the Brothers of Taizé. I had read about the Taizé experience; I was curious not only about the Brothers but also about the individuals and groups who gathered to pray, sing, study and reflect. There I met the founder, Brother Roger Schultz, and dined in silence with the Taizé community.

Since then, I have visited traditional places of pilgrimage dedicated to the Virgin Mary, including Lourdes, France; Czestochowa, Poland; and Fatima, Portugal. I have found my way to the "church" of the anchoress Dame Julian of Norwich in Norwich,

England; the Cathedral of Chartres, France, with its sacred well, crypts and rose windows; England's Canterbury Cathedral; Spain's Santiago de Compostella, the end point for many of the great European pilgrimages; and other places large and small. Each of these journeys made a lasting impression on me, forcing me to open myself to what God asks of me.

English is the only language I speak; in all but the English-speaking areas I visited, I had to point, ask for help or just hope I was doing the right thing. I was blessed with many guides, but my lack of language skills gave me rich experiences of vulnerability and interconnectedness, which are part of being a pilgrim.

While my travels took me to some well-known places, they also led me to living and ancient monasteries and to the incredibly beautiful part of Turkey called Cappadocia, where Christians built chapels laced with icons painted in the soft stone caves of the area; Ireland; the Isle of Iona, off the coast of Scotland; and the islands of Lerins and Malta, in the Mediterranean Sea. In each of these places, something of the grandeur of God is revealed that has widened my vision of life.

Although the woman quoted at the beginning of this section said, "I am not sitting. I am on a journey," in fact much of the spiritual journey happens through sitting – through being quiet and allowing the voice of God to break into our busy lives. In fact, this may be the hardest part of pilgrimage. It's not just in the seeing: more important, it's in the listening. Sometimes the only way transformation can occur is if we sit silently and allow the inner journey to unfold.

As a former student and teacher of English literature, I have long been fascinated by the Middle English writer Geoffrey Chaucer. In the prologue to his masterpiece, *The Canterbury Tales*, he introduces us to the pilgrims and sets the context for their journey to pay their respects to the martyr Thomas Becket, who is entombed in Canterbury Cathedral. Chaucer masterfully reveals the life stories, personalities and motivations of those gathered for the pilgrimage, revealing a cross-section of society.

Ever since I read Chaucer in high school, I have been intrigued by the motivations and stories of people on a journey. For years, I have been fascinated by religious pilgrimage and all that goes into it. I grew up in rural Iowa; my earliest pilgrimage was to the grotto at nearby West Bend. The images of the grotto are distant memories, but the religious significance is not. A sense of God's presence permeated the place and the people there.

At one time, many years ago, I sought funding for research on the relationship of pilgrimage to personal and religious transformation. I wanted to understand what motivates people on their personal search and to study the rebirth of vowed religious life. I didn't get the funding, but the question provided a starting point for me to explore the impact of pilgrimage on the lives of pilgrims. What's more, it forced me to look inside and discover my own journey in a very intentional manner.

Within the Christian tradition, some of the earliest journeys were to the tombs of the early Christian martyrs outside the walls of Rome. Later, Christians made pilgrimages to the tombs of various saints and holy people, such as St. Martin of Tours in France, or St. James the Apostle in Santiago de Compostella, Spain. Countless people still travel to these sites, as well as to the tombs of many others: Brother André in Montreal, Francis of Assisi, and Archbishop Oscar Romero in San Salvador. Likewise, people in the Jewish, Hindu, Islamic and Buddhist traditions travel to the gravesites, tombs and houses of their holy people. In travelling to these places, pilgrims sense the power of the holy. If they can, they touch the tombs, leave messages and flowers, and sit in quiet reflection as a way to meet the saint and touch the sacred.

The religious pilgrimage has the power to connect us to an experience that is bigger than us. Through a variety of experiences – ritual, movement, comfort and discomfort, sharing stories with fellow pilgrims along the way, and quiet reflection – life changes. Sometimes this change is subtle; at other times, it opens us to a new vision of life within us and in the world around us. The late Dom Helder Camara of Brazil once wrote about the challenge of the pilgrim:

Pilgrim
When your ship
long moored in harbour
gives you the illusion
of being a house;
when your ship begins to
put down roots
in the stagnant water
by the quay
PUT OUT TO SEA!
Save your boat's journeying soul
and your own pilgrim soul
cost what it may.

The thoughts in this book emerged over a number of years, during summer holidays and a six-month sabbatical, through observations, journal entries and reflections on my life.

While I chose certain locations ahead of time, sometimes my plans changed as a result of the people I met and what I encountered along the way. The life of a pilgrim, I learned, is filled with surprises, disappointments, comfort and discomfort. Nevertheless, like St. Sarapion the Sindonite, I am a wanderer. I can live no other way.

A friend of mine, Tom Stella, in his book *The God Instinct*, writes, "Solitude is an internal reality. It is less a matter of geography – physical separation from the presence of others – and more about biography being fully present to our true selves. The 'place' of solitude is our heart."[1] I agree. Being a pilgrim is about biography; it's about the heart, often with brief but powerful glimpses of the sacred in the most unusual places. Each of us is invited on a pilgrimage. Some of us must travel to respond to the instinct of the pilgrim. Many of us, however, may never leave our neighbourhoods, yet we will still engage in a life's pilgrimage of great intensity and transformation.

I have sought to make the "inner monk," through both internal and external journeys, the defining image of my life over the years. In fact, the inner and outer journeys are woven together, and one always affects the other.

As you begin this exploration with me, I would like to share a prayer written by Brother Roger, founder of the Taizé community. Taizé was the first place I visited on my first intentional pilgrimage, and I have been there a number of times since then. At Taizé – whether it is at the church, at the meetings or at meals – the spirit of God at work is palpable. There, on a hilltop in a remote part of France, pilgrims gather from all over the world. It is here that I first experienced the collective power of pilgrims and pilgrimage to shape my imagination by song, word, smell, light, colour and candle, word and deed, to listen more attentively to God's voice within me and the assembled community.

> Breath of the love of God,
> for whoever places their trust in you,
> you uncover the wellspring
> from which the unexpected flows.
> Yet sometimes our prayer is so impoverished

it is a sigh, a clumsy language.
But you understand all human expression.
In an inner life that has neither beginning nor
end, you allow us to rest in you, in body and
spirit. Amen.[2]

As this book unfolds, you will discover some of
my glimpses of the sacred. At the beginning of each
chapter, I offer some quotations to help focus your
experience. The end of each chapter offers reflection
questions and food for thought. As you travel along the
road of your own pilgrimage, may your journey be filled
with discovery, peace and the presence of God.

Reflection Questions

1. What outer experiences have given me oppor-
    tunities to think more deeply about life and my
    experience?

2. How have I experienced Saul Alinsky's insight:
    "Change means movement. Movement means
    friction"?

3. How do I discern the goodness or appropriateness
    of a given situation?

4. How have I encountered God in the surprising
    events of daily life?

5. Joan Chittister opens her book *Scarred by Struggle*,
    Transformed by Hope with this statement: "Life is
    a series of lessons, some of them obvious, some of
    them not." What does this statement mean in terms
    of my life experience?

1

The Call to Pilgrimage: Life "Between Dreams"

Hear and understand the instructions which God gave you.—Thomas Merton

There is no formula to teach us how to arrive at maturity and there is no grammar for the language of the inner life.—Dag Hammarskjold

We have what we seek.
We don't have to rush after it.
It was there all the time,
and if we give it time,
it will make itself known to us.
—Thomas Merton

Recently, I was talking with a friend, Riley, who wanted to take a few months off from his busy legal practice to travel and reflect on the direction his life was taking. When he suggested to the senior partners of his prestigious law firm that he wanted a two-month leave of absence, they said, "We can give you a month, but no more." My friend decided to quit his job and seek another one after his travels.

Even though he has highly marketable skills, the choice was difficult. As someone who likes to keep people happy, he did not like the tension that his request and decision generated within the law firm. He wondered if people thought he was crazy for taking time off. He asked me, "Am I nuts?" I said, "No," but I am sure many said yes. Some saw his decision to take time off as career limiting, as something weak. Yet he stood firm and did what he needed to do. To borrow a phrase from philosopher Joseph Campbell, he followed his bliss.

The decision to go away on an extended trip was not made lightly. But he knew he needed the time now to listen deeply to what was moving within him and to look to the road ahead. It was a time to bring closure and healing to some painful events in his life, including a devastating divorce and a lingering uncertainty about where to go next in his personal and professional life.

Though he may not see it that way, my friend is becoming a pilgrim. He is not another tourist off to see the sights, or a deeply religious person; instead, he is on a personal journey filled with risks and uncertainties. While he may be visiting various parts of Europe during his few months off, he is not just any traveller. Behind his journey is a search for something that he may not be able to express in words and may not fully perceive, but he does know that he is not "on tour." His search is connected to something deep within his soul that yearns for healing, clarity of purpose and greater meaning.

Most of us make the private, inner pilgrimage. As we move through life, something springs up from our depths and grabs our attention. We can't dismiss it or shake it off easily. We may be busy in our work, engaged with our families and friends, and connected to many groups, yet we cannot ignore the spirit moving spontaneously within us. We know that if we do ignore it, something in us begins to die. It's a dangerous moment in our lives: one filled with cost that will lead to greater transformation or disfiguring stagnation.

While he could have joined a group pilgrimage to Jerusalem, Iona, Santiago de Compostella or Rome, my friend chose a private journey. In fact, a year earlier he had joined a group going to Italy, but found the routine confining. This time, he wanted to be free to plan his own time. He wanted to be able to pause in Assisi as long as he wished, instead of being limited to the three-hour tour of the site plus a group lunch. (For many, the group experience is an excellent way to travel, be connected with others and find their way through the maze of cities, towns and villages; for others, it is soul-numbing.)

For my friend, pilgrimage meant separation from work, family, friends and familiar patterns of being and doing – something he had not done before. In his case, he opted to take a few months to travel as cheaply as possible through Europe. In doing so, he created an inner space for movement and transformation to occur. There were moments and even days of loneliness where he wondered if he was doing the right thing, but he persisted. We met up in France, spending time in a monastery at Cîteaux, where St. Bernard started the Cistercian order of Benedictines. Then we travelled to the coast of southern France, and on to Paris. It gave each of us time to step back, to check in and see how the journey was going, and to enjoy the solitude of the monastery and the power of the sea in southern France.

In the course of a journey like my friend's, there are moments in which things come together. These moments of clarity often happen when we are walking down a street, experiencing the beauty of nature or friendship, or quietly reflecting. We get a new sense of life and energy. These moments can be neither planned nor expected. They just happen.

For many who travel in a group, shared ritual binds them together and strengthens their own life: for instance, the crowds of people joined in prayer and movement at the shrine at Lourdes, where the sick and the well gather in hopes of healing.

The experience that my friend chose demands some type of solitude and isolation, however. Pilgrims following this path often feel alone and lonely. We wonder, "Am I doing the right thing? Should I have used this money for something else for my family or myself?" Yet, the time I often call "between dreams" gives us a chance to step back, grapple with life's uncertainty and move into a new dimension of our lives.

We all eventually return home. If a genuine pilgrimage has happened, we feel a shift. The change of perspective may not be readily apparent, but gradually something begins to change. Often we cannot explain it, but know we feel more connected to the sacred. The inner pilgrimage often brings us back to the place where we began with new energy and wisdom. We are not the same people who started out on the journey. We awaken to a new sense of purpose and dignity. Thomas Merton captures it well when he reflects,

> What can we gain by sailing to the moon if we are not able to cross the abyss that separates us from ourselves? This is the most important of all voyages of discovery, and without it, all the rest are not only useless, but also disastrous.[3]

A Personal Awakening

Journal – Lake Louise, Alberta

> For some reason, today marks the beginning of a new journey for me. I can feel it in the depth of my bones and soul! I am not sure what that means, but something different is happening within me. Tucked away in a quiet room in Deer Lodge in Lake Louise, Alberta, surrounded by the towering Rocky Mountains and snow-draped evergreen trees, I now realize that something moved within me as I walked in the woods. Whether it was my sudden desire to move away from the noisy guests at the hotel or to avoid the usual pathways, something said "now is the time to be open to something new, and that involves a journey both inwardly and outwardly." Lake Louise is not one of the great pilgrimage sites, like St. Joseph's Oratory in Montreal or the Vézelay Cathedral in France, but it is here, secluded in the mountains of rural Alberta in a room with neither radio nor television, that God urges me to write, reflect and grow.
>
> As I prepared to leave home last night, my eyes fell upon the book *Thomas Merton in Alaska: The Alaskan Conferences, Journals and Letters.* Something within me

said, "Take it, read it and ponder it," and so I did. Skipping the journal entries and the letters, I moved directly to the opening lines of his first conference, entitled "This is God's Work." He reminds his audience that we are called not to our work but to God's work, day in and day out. For me, the journey represents an attempt to discover anew God's call within – as a member of a vowed religious congregation, the Brothers of Holy Cross; as a health-care consultant; and as a teacher of Christian spirituality – and to let my life be God's work. That means not just the "work" that I do, but the very way I live, organize and focus my life.

To be touched by God demands a fresh willingness to let myself be transformed and to rediscover my centre. This means pulling apart again the illusions of power, impact, control and destiny, and rediscovering what I have probably always known: I am loved, cherished and held in God's tender mercy. Yet, right now, nothing is too clear.

The days, weeks, months and years ahead point to this journey of unmasking: making decisions about career and lifestyle and taking time alone to reflect, observe and write. Today marks a beginning...a time alone and a time apart. A time in which the extrovert in me begs for companionship, distraction and busyness, yet the introvert yearns for solitude, stillness and attentiveness. So be it!

Noticing God's presence

I am moved by Thomas Merton's words about the awareness of God's presence in our life. He says, "Contemplation is the realization of God in our life, not just the realization of an idea or something partial, but a realization of the whole thing – the realization that we belong totally to God and God has

24

given God's self totally to us."[4] As I wrestle with these words and let them sink into my consciousness, I realize how far away I am from a felt awareness of God's presence. Yet I know deep down, through faith and past experience, that God continues to dwell within me. I just cannot feel it. Instead, I experience a deep void of affect and awareness.

As I walk on a fresh trail among the stately evergreens covered in new snow, and look up at the glaciers and incredible mountains, the stark beauty of God's creation is ever present. Yet when I look into my heart and reflect upon my actions, attitudes and values, I sense a great distance and alienation from the sacred. Illness has certainly helped to ground me. Being forbidden to travel by air for a few months because of a blood clot in my leg has forced me to realign my life and re-examine how I spend my time and energy.

When I went to a holistic health centre in Chicago a few months ago, before this new blood clot, to do some research on the connection between body, mind and soul, I used my own experience of having had a blood clot. The doctor I met with said that besides giving me the traditional medication for the problem, he would ask me to identify what is stuck in my life, and encourage me to find time for prayer and regular meditation. When I could pinpoint where I was stuck, there might be a new opening. I can only trust that this will be the case. Something is stirring within me, and I cannot block it out. If I do, I fear that my life will be endangered and I will have missed something important that I needed to embrace.

As I reflect in the stillness of the forest pathways, I sense that being a pilgrim for me right now is a coming home. I am allowing God to touch once again both the light and the darkness within me and to say, "Peace, I am with you." This peace that God offers exists not only in my soul, but also in my relationships, work and creativity. I am rediscovering Merton's words: "Perhaps I am stronger than I think. Perhaps I am afraid of my strength and turn it against myself to make myself weak. Perhaps I am most afraid of the strength of God within me."[5]

Peace has been absent from my life for so long; I have manically rushed from one project to another, from one experience to another. I have been acting like Superman, but I am not Superman. I cannot change everything, nor can I control everything: this is one lesson I am learning quickly. I cannot even heal myself, never mind fix all the problems at work.

Now, through the blood clots in my leg, I am being forced to come home again to what is important in my life as a Brother, teacher and Christian health-care consultant. Pilgrimage is both an inner and an outer journey to wholeness and holiness. Deer Lodge, with its rustic charm and snow-covered roofs in the shadow of Victoria Glacier and Lake Louise, provides a place of repose, rediscovery and new beginnings. I am lucky to be here.

An invitation to listen to the "inner monk"

It's clear that something deep inside me is inviting me to become quiet, to listen. My entire inner self is telling me to stop and listen to what is important, instead of getting involved in all the ups and downs of work and the politics of my religious community. I joined Holy Cross sight unseen as a seventeen-year-old high school graduate, and it is both a defining and core element of who I am today.

Part of the journey now unfolding within me is to serve and care for the monk within, and to create the solitude and stillness my inner monk needs to mature and to express himself. Is this what is blocked in me?

Ever since I heard the phrase "the monk within," during a retreat at a monastery in northern California for people engaged in social and peace ministries, a bell of recognition and challenge has been ringing inside me. It intrigues me intellectually, but it's more than that. The monk leading the retreat was not talking about professed monks with vows of poverty, celibacy, obedience and, often, stability. Instead, he was referring to the work of Raimundo Panikkar, who wrote *Blessed Simplicity: The Monk as Universal Archetype.*

I read once that Aristotle talked about three components of our lives: action, enjoyment and contemplation. For me, the journey needs to be about solitude, stillness, receptivity and wonder. It demands the same intensity as all the outer travel I have been doing for my job. But now, the tables are turned and the invitation is before me. Free the inner monk. Find the solitude and stillness you need to usher in the next stage of your life. A voice seems to be saying, "You now know the destiny and the direction. Choose it and choose life, not death." The invitation is connected to the third element Aristotle listed: the life of contemplation that lives within all of us but is often lost amidst lives of action and enjoyment.

The challenge goes against so many of my well-established patterns. Being on the road or flying somewhere every week is taking its toll on me. My first diagnosed blood clot, or deep vein thrombosis (DVT), was in England, where I was visiting a friend. (I am sure I had an earlier one, but the strong medication I got from a physician in a walk-in clinic hid the symptoms for a while.) My most recent one was diagnosed right before I was to leave for the airport to go to Iowa for the Christmas holidays. Yet, in between, I have been all over North America doing workshops, going to meetings and teaching classes. I guess it's harder to save my own soul than to try and save the "souls" of the organizations that I allow to devour so much of my energy. Just giving my soul the attention, focus and energy that I give my outer work will change the course of my life.

I have to admit that I am a monk at heart. The longing is strong, the call for contemplation and solitude urgent, but somehow I do not seem to be able to find a way to live a more harmonious life. I am not just another businessman living on the road most of the time. The very roots of the vocation of a Brother within the Catholic Church, which I chose many years ago, flows from the monastic tradition. The monk's calling is to be whole and attentive to following God's voice in all aspects of daily life.

I have constant work, noise, travel and move-ment to block, avoid, shield and distract myself from concretely expressing a deeper part of my life. The world of action and experience makes it easy for me to numb the ache inside. Now I must refocus myself to follow wherever this inner urge is going to lead me. Recently I wrote the following statement about my work and myself for a Holy Cross publication. I wonder now how true it is. Am I deluding myself?

The Irish have a word in Gaelic, Grieshog, which is the process of burying warm coals in the night in order to preserve the fire for the cold mor-ning to come. They save the day's fire in order to have a fast-starting fire the next day. The process is extremely important. For if the coals go out, a new fire must be built in the morning, a time-consuming process.

My work in Christian health care can best be described as attending to the "coals" and "fire" of Christian faith-based health care and making sure that they do not go out. Whether it be through workshops, board retreats, strategic planning, leadership programs, editing a magazine or planning conferences for faith-based health-care organizations in Alberta or other parts of Canada, attending to the "fire" of Christian health care and its voice and mission within a publicly funded and universal system of health-care delivery dominates my life.

As a ministry that I basically fell into, it has provided me with a unique sense of how God works through intuitions, impulses and the invitation of others. This ministry has allowed me to see growth, transformation and a deepening of what it means to be Christian/faith-based organizations in a society driven more by financial planning than service.
At the end of the day, as the journey unfolds, I need to keep asking myself: Is this what God is asking of me? Is this how I am to live my life as monk, Brother, educator and consultant? How do I allow the right things to unfold in my life? How do I trust that God walks with me?

The cost of integrity

Time to head back home to Edmonton. It's a slow process: driving for 45 minutes, then stopping, getting out and stretching my legs to prevent another blood clot. If nothing else, this discipline slows me down, allows me to walk a bit and stop and smell the roses – except now it's the crisp air of winter that I smell.

The snow has been falling ever since first light. The sky is grey, but with all the fresh snow coming down and the occasional cross-country skier passing by, the picture is one of integrated and harmonious beauty. The first stop on the unexpected pilgrimage has helped me realize that from now on, I need to be as attentive to my inner world as I am to the outer world. This is going to be difficult. I resist all the way. I find it easy to talk and write about listening and responding, about change, but making myself available to my inner self is hard work. As an extrovert and workaholic, I don't relish it. But what choice do I have? The urge within me is poignant and requires attention. I need to rediscover the essential elements in my life and let go of all that distracts from who I am as a monk. I have been especially struck by Carl Jung's remarks:

Everything good is costly, and the development of personality is one of the most costly of all things. It is a matter of saying yes to oneself, of taking oneself as the most serious of tasks, of being conscious of everything one does, and keeping it constantly before one's eyes in all its dubious aspects...truly a task that taxes us to the utmost.[6]

Jung captures in psychological terms the essence of what German theologian and martyr Dietrich Bonhoeffer captures in theological terms when he writes of costly grace and the cost of discipleship. Discipleship means not only doing as Jesus did, which even he found difficult at times, but also allowing God's healing grace, compassion and love to be free within me and lead me. Thus, discipleship demands both an inner and outer disciplined attentiveness to God's presence and voice. That's not easy, at least for me! I am very disciplined when it comes to work, but otherwise, discipline is not my strong suit. I sense a major struggle ahead, but I don't have a choice. I just don't want any more blood clots! They are dangerous and since they are silent, they can kill easily. A stroke or heart attack could easily destroy me, so I need to be vigilant. Also, given the fact that I have had two or three blood clots in the last few months, my entire system of clotting has stopped working. I am on daily doses of a blood thinner to control the clotting. This medication needs to be monitored through frequent blood tests to make sure my blood does not get too thin or too thick.

The days here at Lake Louise have been surprisingly insightful, challenging and restful. I cannot help but reflect on the powerful words of Francis of Assisi: "How do I hear the voice of Jesus and how do I follow him on the way even when that way leads to the cross?"[7]

The Call to Be a Pilgrim

The old man was hardly under the ground when Robert announced to his mother and sister that nothing could stop him from setting out on his pilgrimage to Rome, to satisfy his urge and atone for his and his father's sins. In vain the women complained; in vain they scolded. He remained stubborn, and instead of taking care of them...he set out on his journey.... he was driven mainly by a desire to travel, and to this was added a kind of superficial piety.... he stayed away for a year or more....[8]

The call to be a pilgrim, to explore both inwardly and outwardly, can occur anytime in our lives. For some, like Robert in Herman Hesse's novel *Narcissus and Goldmund*, it may stem from a need to make amends for their sins. This type of call can be strong, compelling, filled with mixed motives. For others, it might be gentler. Robert was inspired by the traditional lore of the pilgrimage to Rome, but also felt the desire to travel. We are often no different. The lure of the road, the unknown and the questions lurking in our souls push us forward onto uncharted paths.

Our motivations are never completely pure; our decisions are often based on a mixture of reasons. Yet, being on the road and removed from daily rituals, companions and settings can provide the space for inner exploration if we let it. The choice is ours. We hear the call of the inner pilgrim, yet deciding to surrender to the call is fraught with difficulty. After the initial surge of energy, we watch as fear, loneliness, old patterns and a range of vicissitudes test our willingness to say yes to the call. My journals are filled with good intentions: often, though, when the going gets tough, I fall back into my well-worn ways of being.

For many, the call demands an inner transformation, a letting go of images of who we are and how we express ourselves. For others, the inner transformation is coupled with a need to get away, to explore new places so we can answer the call. However we hear the summons, it is up to us to respond – or not. No one else can respond for us. We need to move with courage and action. If we avoid the summons, we choose to live the status quo, something the soul abhors. W.H. Auden says it best in his poem "The Age of Anxiety," where he reflects upon the struggle to shun the status quo and move into the unknown. His words are haunting and telling:

> We would rather be ruined than changed;
> We would rather die in our dread
> Than climb the cross of the moment
> And let our illusions die.

The choice to say yes, to let go of our fears and embrace the largeness of our being, has consequences. The questions that confront us in both our waking moments and in our dreams are these: Am I willing to allow the pilgrim within me to go on the journey needed for my wholeness and salvation? If so, what might the consequences be for me and for others? Am I willing and able to trust in the providence of God? Do I, in the midst of my life, discern God's loving hand?

Reflection Questions

1. "Everything good is costly, and the development of personality is one of the most costly of all things. It is a matter of saying yes to oneself, of taking oneself as the most serious of tasks, of being conscious of everything one does, and keeping it constantly before one's eyes in all its dubious aspects…truly a task that taxes us to the utmost." In what ways do these words of Carl Jung speak to me?

2. How have I been awakened to my call in life recently?

3. How have I responded to God's call?

Food for Thought

Once you have an inner knowledge of your true vocation, you have a point of orientation. That will help you decide what to do and what to let go of, what to say and what to remain silent about, when to go out and when to stay home, who to be with and who to avoid.... God does not require of you what is beyond your ability, what leads you away from God, or what makes you depressed or sad. God wants you to live for others and to live that presence well.—Henri Nouwen

How do we find our vocation? In the end, it is through the capacity of the ego to forgo its need for security and comfort in service to some deeper force. But this is not easy.—James Hollis

2

Pilgrimage: The Ins and Outs

Pilgrim: 1. A person who journeys to a sacred place for religious reasons 2. A wanderer or traveller (root: Middle English *pilegrim* from Provençal *pelegrin* from Latin *peregrinus, stranger*)

Pilgrimage: 1. A pilgrim's journey 2. Life viewed as a journey 3. Any journey taken for nostalgic or sentimental reasons—*Canadian Oxford Dictionary*

Five Excellent Practices of Pilgrimages

- Practice the arts of attention and listening
- Practice renewing yourself every day
- Practice meandering toward the centre of every place
- Practice the ritual of reading sacred texts
- Practice gratitude and praise-singing.
  —inspired by a fifth-century conversation between Zin Zhang and Confucius[9]

Getting Going: Some Journal Entries

Czestochowa, Poland

I have often talked about pilgrimage and disorientation in my classes at the university. Well, today proved to be a disorienting day. As many frustrations as possible manifested themselves, and I discovered how impatient I can get. The chapel and church were crowded, with people kneeling and praying all over the place. What was happening? What is the great attraction? Today I don't know.

My clothes are terribly dirty and tomorrow is another travel day. When we get back, we can relax, but then we visit the death camps in Auschwitz on one day and Warsaw on another. There is a lot of moving around, yet on the whole I feel good about the trip. It is certainly all new to me and I would be miserable if I were trying to do this alone. It's almost essential to be with someone else to share the ups and downs and to find my way in this foreign environment.

Newmarket, England

It's almost time to leave here. This has been a good stop because I needed to rest and to get grounded. It was good to see my friend again. I could not get centred with everyone in London and all the activity that accompanies living with a family. So, this stay in Newmarket was really good. I am a little worried about the feeling of tension in my chest – it's nothing new but I still worry.

Inner voice: You need to respect your voice, your soul and your calling to be a monk, a writer and a Brother. You are not here to be tourist, host, gadfly, drinker, etc. Honour your calling as monk and things will work out. You don't have to keep fighting me and my call; instead, you need to trust in my love for you. I know it's very difficult, but try!

Tom: I am going to try. But how?

Inner voice: First, give yourself more time and focus in prayer. Honour your calling from deep within yourself and nurture it. Do not fear it; honour it. This is soul time, remember. It's a time for stillness, listening, gratitude and contemplation, not accumulating more unconnected experiences. Second, sit in real stillness each day and let my grace rush over you. Third, dialogue with me and with others, write in these journals and keep centred.

Tom: I will try.

Two days later

I've been here in Newmarket for two days now, and I feel like I need to come to grips with my purpose for travelling to the UK. I know it is not to engage in idle chitchat, to tour empty places and visit poets' graves. It's a time to reclaim my soul and voice. I think some of the tension I feel in my chest and throat has to do with claiming my voice and what I desire and need. But what do I need? I need to be still and remember that God is trying to break through in my life in a new way. I need to make room for God in the quiet of my heart, rather than just talking about it. I need to remind myself that at the core of my being is the desire to be an artist, a writer, a friend and a monk: all of these want to be recognized and revered.

Tomorrow, I head off for York, in the north of England. I must articulate what I need during this time of pilgrimage – solitude and healing – instead of pretending that others can guess it. Finally, I must respect myself, not sabotage my journey by caring for others instead of myself.

So, I am on the move again. I will have three days in Iona and three in Glastonbury with some time in the west of Ireland as well as on the Holy Isle of Lindisfarne. I know not much is left there, but even touching the holy ground is important for me.

Lindisfarne

The beauty of the environment here is overwhelming. I still don't feel like I am on pilgrimage, but once I get to Iona and then onto Glastonbury, I expect I will feel I am journeying with you, Lord, and feel the call to holiness. Lindisfarne (Holy Island) has taught me that holiness can be achieved by letting go and trusting in God's abiding love, just as the Irish monks who settled here had to trust that this was where God was leading them. The letting go and trusting for me is subtle. It's about not trying to plan everything, to control everything (something I really like to do), but allowing myself to be struck by the awe and mystery of life. The island also reminded me that life is about doing good works well: caring for people, being kind and forgiving, and allowing grace to flow deeply through all of us. The subtle beauty and solitude of the isle reminds me to restore order, depth and beauty in my soul.

If my mission is spiritual, then I need solitude, attentiveness and compassion in my life. And yes, even though it is hard to say and write, I need to abandon myself and trust in your pervasive love and proddings. May your beauty grow within me and through all those who come into my life. Amen.

The Way of the Pilgrim

Once my mother asked me, "Why do you go to Europe so often?" I replied (with some guilt for not going to rural Iowa to see her more often) that I was writing a book and needed to be in certain places. Plus, I have thousands of frequent flyer points because I travel so much for work, so I never have to pay for the trip. My answer was only partly true. The main reason I go, and go often, is that something pulls me to explore places of holiness and transformation.

In various university classes in which I have taught spirituality, I often talked about pilgrimage. Something about this subject always ignited the souls of the students. While we never did a pilgrimage together, each group showed a profound desire to reflect on their lives in greater depth and someday make a pilgrimage to a sacred place. They saw that their lives were moving in ways that were often surprising and mysterious; the idea of pilgrimage provided a way to explore their experiences inwardly as well as outwardly.

While most of the pilgrimages we make are inward bound, sometimes they also have an outward expression. The reasons for going on a pilgrimage are as varied as the people who do them, but certain themes emerge. While the tourist may go to the same place to see the outer reality, the pilgrim is focused on the inner and symbolic reality of the place.

I have noticed over and over again that most people do not take the time to stop and get a sense of a place. I watch the crowds flow through a great cathedral, such as Chartres, take pictures, move up and down the aisles, point out the rose windows, search for the labyrinth on the floor, and move on to the next attraction. Rarely do people sit and allow the place to speak to them. Too often, we miss the mystery and sacredness. Unfortunately, many people and travel groups have become consumers of the sacred places in our midst. The crowds of tourists following their tour guide around the great sacred spots of antiquity only diminish the sacredness of a place. These "hot spots" of tourist travel on busy schedules filled with action and experience are short on contemplation.

Some Reasons for a Pilgrimage

Why do people go on a religious pilgrimage? First, we like to go to a place where something has happened of special significance to us and our faith tradition. For example, Jews, Christians and Muslims travel to Jerusalem; each seeks something different there. As Sir Steven Runciman, who wrote on the Crusades, says, "The desire to be a pilgrim is deeply rooted in human nature, to stand where those that we reverence once stood, to see the very sites where they were born and toiled and died, gives us a feeling of mystical contact with them and is a practical expression of our homage."[10]

A desire for healing or a sense of wholeness is a second reason many embark upon a pilgrimage. This desire for healing takes many different forms. For some, it is atonement for their sins. Whether it be a Muslim undertaking the Hajj, a Jew praying at the Western Wall or a Christian walking the Via Dolorosa, pilgrims know they need forgiveness and mercy. In many cases, healing means a cure from illness or distress. People go to Lourdes in search of a physical cure, but often what they find there is spiritual healing – a state of coming to a deeper sense of wholeness about their lives. Michael Kearney MD writes, "Soul pain is the experience of an individual who has become disconnected and alienated from the deepest and most fundamental aspects of himself or herself."[11] Lac Ste. Anne, Alberta, is a place of pilgrimage for Aboriginal people who wade into the lake in search of healing and cure. Some people want to touch the tomb of a holy person who was known for a healing presence; touch is the most basic form of communication.

A third reason for going on pilgrimage is to give thanks for a favour granted. Not long ago, while I was at the shrine dedicated to Mary in Fatima, I watched people under a glaring, unrelenting sun approach on their knees the shrine where Mary is said to have appeared to three peasant children. Old and young crawled – some with babies in their arms, some supported by friends or relatives – towards the shrine. When I mentioned this experience to a friend, she said her mother had done that after the birth of her brother. Her mother had promised to make the journey halfway around the world to Fatima and approach the shrine on her knees if her pregnancy went well and she gave birth to a son. In many of the major pilgrimage sites, one sees tokens of appreciation inscribed on the walls or mountains of canes and crutches left behind.

A fourth, and perhaps the most common, reason for a pilgrimage is to express one's love for God. A Jewish colleague once told me that for him, going to Jerusalem was a deeply religious experience of God's love. Throughout history, people have walked across Europe, flocked to Medina in Saudi Arabia, gone to a local shrine or sat quietly in a sacred place to commune with

God and express their gratitude and love. St. Augustine wrote, "You have made us for yourself, O God, and our hearts are restless until they rest in you."

A fifth reason that people make a pilgrimage is to explore their lives. Often we have no idea why we begin an inner or outer journey, but we do it anyway. Something within us says "Go." Religious history is filled with stories of a call awakening this impulse within a person. In the Hebrew Scriptures, Abram and Sara follow God's call to go to a new land. Moses answers the call to lead the Israelites out of Egypt. Jonah heeds the call to preach to the people of Nineveh.

Sixth, many sense that through the journey they can reconnect to fragmented, broken or forgotten parts of themselves. All of us need to step outside our usual pace every now and then. Sometimes a relaxing weekend away is enough, but at other times, we need to be more focused. Something has been lost or abandoned, perhaps due to a break in a relationship, a crisis at work, a lack of balance and harmony, or a sense of homelessness at the core of our being. Through the pilgrim journey, the time we spend outside our usual environment, we have more time to reflect, and some of the broken pieces of ourselves come back together again. We realize that if we are to find a new harmony in our lives, we must change how we live and seek more coherence between our inner and outer selves.

Pilgrimage, whether with groups or alone, whether to a faraway place or close to home, demands patience, perseverance and openness. Where the journey will lead no one knows, for the essence of being a pilgrim, both inwardly and outwardly, is being surprised by God and led in a direction that is more in keeping with who we are called to be.

I have never gone on a group pilgrimage; perhaps because I spend so much of my time with people, I prefer the solo journey. But I still share with other people these same six main reasons for becoming a pilgrim. In my pilgrimage journey, I have felt clearly my need to know myself, others and God more fully, and to better understand the roots of religious renewal and transformation.

Reflection Questions

1. In what ways have I experienced the call of the pilgrim?
2. For me, being a pilgrim and being on a pilgrimage means...
3. Joseph Campbell invites us to "follow our bliss" or call: what does that mean for me?

Food for Thought

In our era, the road to holiness necessarily passes through the world of action.—Dag Hammarskjold

The danger always remains that you will let other people run away with your sacred centre, thus throwing you into anguish.... It might take a great deal of time and discipline to fully reconnect your deep, hidden self and your public self, which is known, loved, and accepted but also criticized by the world. Gradually, though, you will begin feeling more connected and become more fully who you are – a child of God. There lies your true freedom.—Henri Nouwen

The late Joseph Campbell stated, we have to "follow our bliss"…find something that wholly involves and enthralls us, even if it seems hopelessly unfashionable and unproductive, and throw ourselves into this, heart and soul…but that bliss provides us with a clue: if we follow it to the end, it will take us to the heart of life. —Karen Armstrong

3

Chance Encounters

Chance (noun and verb): 1. A possibility 2. A risk 3. An unplanned occurrence/the absence of design or discoverable cause 4. An opportunity 5. The way things happen.— *Canadian Oxford Dictionary*

Dear Lord, help me remember that nothing is going to happen to me today that You and I can't handle together. Amen.—Jo Sullivan Coyle

Open my eyes, so that I may behold wondrous things.—Psalm 119:18

When I was crossing into Gaza, I was asked at the checkpoint whether I was carrying any weapons. I replied: "Oh yes, my prayer books."—Mother Teresa

Who among us has not had an experience of bumping into someone who has awakened us to a deeper aspect of our lives? Perhaps we struck up a conversation with a stranger and discovered an answer to a question that had been troubling us for a long time. Maybe we saw someone we had not seen in years and, bang, we connected and integration happened.

Being on pilgrimage has a lot to do with chance encounters. If we travel alone, we depend on others to interpret for us, tell us what we are eating, and translate our needs and points of view. We may stray into a place, feel a connection and stay for a while. We may meet people along the way who have a message for us, if we can hear it.

These chance encounters reveal possibilities and opportunities we cannot plan and would not usually experience. Yet there are also risks. For one thing, we may be in a foreign country. We may not know our way, understand the language or be aware of the local customs. There may be pickpockets, difficult people and dangers. But one of the biggest risks is this: we might just get what we seek. We could find ourselves changed, and that is a very real part of the journey. During pilgrimage, we create a new space internally and may not be able to return to our old ways. We must be willing to live with some uncertainty and trust that the right things will happen according to God's plans for us; otherwise, we can be frozen in a certain time and place. This is true whether the pilgrimage is inner or outer. We cannot avoid risk, but we can trust in God's guiding presence, our own common sense and the essential goodness of others.

Part 1: Mont Saint-Michel, France

In Celtic mythology, the island of Mont Saint-Michel on the Normandy coast of northern France was remembered as one of the sea tombs into which the dead were conveyed. According to legend, in 708 AD, St. Michel appeared to Aubert, Bishop of Avranches, and instructed him to build a devotional chapel on the top of the mount. In 966, Richard I, Duke of Normandy, gave Mont Saint-Michel to the Benedictine monks to create a centre of learning. Later, it was used as a military garrison, at the disposal of both the abbot and the king. During the Hundred Years War against England in the fifteenth century, the mount remained French. Today, a small monastic community lives there. Guests are welcome to stay at the monastery if they participate in the prayer, meals and silence of the community.

Journal: Finding a community

It's amazing what touches the soul. Here I am at Mont Saint-Michel, the great fortress and abbey on the north coast of France. It's hot and crowded. As I walk through the throngs of tourists – it might be more accurate to say, as I pushed and was pushed – on the street leading up to the abbey church, I can't help but wonder, why are people here? More important, why am I here? Is it just to check out the site for next year's pilgrimage group from St. Stephen's College at the University of Alberta, or does this place have a message for me?

I can't say what moved all the people in the lanes and streets to come here. Certainly, the majesty of the place, which is surrounded by water, overpowers people when they come upon it. The walk to the abbey and church, built at the very top of the mount, demands both stamina and commitment. On this hot July holiday weekend, the narrow, medieval lanes are crammed with people of all ages climbing up and down. Some push or carry babies, strollers and small children. Many people are walking with their dogs. Elderly pilgrims walk one step at a time, slowly but surely, resting periodically at the various lookout spots. How do all these people do it? Something must be compelling them to climb up and up and up.

Part of the allure of getting to the top of Mont Saint-Michel is the physical challenge. Will I make it to the top? And, if I do, what will I find? In my case, I found a community. They opened the door, said welcome, and ushered me into a dining room where the community and a few guests were finishing the noon meal. They offered some dessert and wine; I gladly accepted, and I relaxed.

When everyone was finished eating, we wound our way through several narrow stairways and rooms into a small chapel for mid-afternoon prayer. There, in the silence of the oratory, we quieted ourselves. Like our ancestors who gathered in this place over the centuries, we chanted some psalms, listened to a short reading from the Bible, prayed for the world and sat in silence. Then, quietly, we left. I was shown to a room with a few beds in it and told that if more pilgrims arrived, I might have to share the room with others. After I unpacked, I tried to get my bearings. At first, I felt completely lost among the stairwells, turns and closed rooms but eventually found my way through the maze. I located the exit and went outside again into life in the lanes and shops of Mont Saint-Michel.

Looking up at more stairs, I was tempted to say "no way," but I climbed up to the very top and looked around. The hordes of tourists were over-whelming. Back in the village, I entered the parish church, Saint-Pierre. Suddenly, with the warmth from the banks of candles burning in front of the altar, with the Archangel Michael crushing the head of the dragon, and more candles flickering in front of the Virgin and child, a sense of peace embraced me. Something of the mystery and awe of the place touched me deeply. Despite the music rehearsal that

God's preserve

48

was underway and the people walking through, deep reverence and sacredness filled that place.

Unlike the great church at the top of the hill, or the oratory tucked away inside the abbey, the parish church smelled and felt holy. The warmth of the candles, the brilliant colours of the statues and the wall hanging behind the main altar, the intimacy of the church all revealed the tender presence of God. I had a sense of coming home, of being found and welcomed again. It was good.

I came to Mont Saint-Michel to feel God's presence in the grandeur of the citadel, but was confounded. God uses small things to grab my attention.

An Accidental Pilgrim

On my last night at evening prayer at Mont Saint-Michel, I noticed a new face across from me in the chapel: a man, tanned, early fifties, wearing flip-flops, a blue T-shirt with a small cross around his neck, and lime-green pants. At first I thought he was a worker who decided to join us for evening prayer before the church closed, but at dinner he introduced himself to me as a pilgrim. His name was Jean-Pierre.

Over dinner, Jean-Pierre mentioned that he had spent the past ten days walking in France from Rouen to Mont Saint-Michel. I asked him how long he was going to stay, and he replied, "Until God tells me to move on." When I asked if he was going to walk back home, he said, "No, my wife will come and fetch me." Later that evening, I saw him walking in the garden with a visiting elderly monk, but did not have a chance to talk to him again until the next morning, when we were both looking for the entrance gate back into the abbey. As we searched for the wooden door that opened onto a series of stairways to the abbey, I asked him if we could talk. We agreed to meet around 9:00 p.m.

At evening prayer, he was again sitting across from me. As I looked down at his feet, I noticed white bandages on a couple of his toes. One of the bandages revealed a fresh bloodstain. Blisters, probably. He has to be uncomfortable, I thought. I had a few aches and pains from climbing the hundreds of stairs, but this man was bleeding.

The pilgrim Jean-Pierre is a photographer, husband and father of two who at age 49 awakened by sheer coincidence to God's presence in his life. He and some other photographers decided to photograph a monastery near where they lived. After the shoot, he asked to stay a little longer. Then he decided to stay for a week.

For over 30 years, God, spirituality and prayer had not been part of his life. Then, in the quiet of the chapel one evening, he got an overpowering sense of God's love for him. At first he thought, "I am a sinner; it must be for someone else." Realizing he was alone in the chapel, he felt the love of Christ pour into his heart and reawaken in him God's personal and alluring love for him.

Ever since then, he has stayed as often as possible in monasteries rather than hotels during his travels. Monasteries provide him with a venue that values solitude, prayer and community. The very essence of a monastery is to create space for one to be aware of God in all things. Within the context of the monastery, Jean-Pierre has found a place that allows him to refocus his energy, step back from his busy life as a fashion photographer and attend more closely to God's ongoing call in his life.

His decision to make a pilgrimage stemmed from his prayer and a feeling that God was calling him to do it. With no money in his pockets, he left home to walk to Mont Saint-Michel. He had no predetermined place to stay or eat, but what he needed – "just what I needed," he said – appeared along the way. "Some gave me food and shelter because I was a pilgrim," he told me. "Others wrote in my pilgrimage book, asked me to pray for them and their intentions, and gave me a little money to buy some food." He added, "While I had chosen the roads, like with any pilgrimage, things change, and God leads. I zigzagged back and forth, but on each part of the journey here, God provided."

As we sat talking and relaxing at the top of the abbey steps looking over the ocean, the evening sun peeking out from behind the clouds, I could not help but be amazed and humbled to meet someone whose face shone with the love of God. Not only did Jean-Pierre share with me his story, he shared his trust in God's providence and revealed how providence continually manifests itself in his life. I wish my faith could be as clear and as trusting.

As the sun started to set, the sound and light show was in the abbey and its environs. Walking inside the church, which was illuminated by recessed lighting on the floor and the pillars and by large candles forming a column of light on both sides of the church, listening to the medieval music and Gregorian chant around me, I marvelled at the mysterious ways in which God touches our hearts and moves our minds.

In the morning, I walked out the back door of the abbey kitchen and prepared to go down the stairs to the ramparts surrounding the citadel to catch my bus to the train station. There beside the door, tucked into the corner, was Jean-Pierre's pilgrim staff and bundle. I guess it was time for him to continue his journey.

Journal: Departure and discovery

> I am just about ready to leave Mont Saint-Michel. As I sit here in my room with the morning sun just breaking through the clouds, the view of the surrounding area is breathtaking. It has been a good experience, but I am ready to move on. I guess it's the restless pilgrim within me. Also, I have a long journey today to the south of France and St. Raphael.
>
> During the last few days, as I walked up the narrow, twisting steps and through the lanes of the village, I wondered how they got all the goods they need into the cafés, restaurants, bars and shops. Well, I found out this morning as I sat against the ancient walls and waited for the 9:00 bus. By 8:20 a.m., the parking lot outside the gates was bustling: not only with tourists and pilgrims of every age and nationality, but also with purveyors of various goods and services.

Off to the left, produce, food, cartons of milk and other goods were stacked waiting for a tractor with a lift to fetch them. Empty cartons were brought out of the village, and stacks of full ones went in, each with a destination written on its side. Then the fish sellers arrived, carrying their catches in big plastic bags. Bread was being unloaded at the same time. Some of it was carried in huge sacks by an older man, while a middle-aged woman pushed a big yellow cart filled with bags of fresh bread. A young schoolboy carried round loaves in his hands.

Not to be outdone, Brinks Security arrived in black Mercedes-Benz vehicles with pistol-clutching guards who walked through the gates to collect the money from the banks. Then it was time for the butcher, the ice-cream truck, the people with clean white tablecloths and napkins, and on and on it went. How does a village get fed? By ordinary people doing ordinary things.

Not only do our stomachs need to be fed, our eyes also need care. Early in the morning, before many of the tour buses and groups started parading through the gates, men in blue work uniforms were sweeping, raking and washing the streets and walkways. Cigarette butts, food wrappers, animal droppings and scattered pieces of paper were removed. Then the ancient beauty of stones and water came together to give quiet praise to a God revealed through the simple things of life.

Part 2: Vézelay, France

I am staying in the old infirmary of the monastery, which has been turned into a boutique, a guesthouse, a home and a café. I have only one night here, and then I will move into a hotel next to the Church of the Magdalene. *The Guide for Pilgrims to Santiago in*

Compostella says, "Pilgrim to Compostella, what you confided to us on leaving the church of Saint James can well apply to the church of the Magdalene. He who arrives with a heavy heart leaves happy and consoled after contemplating the splendid perfection of the Church." And then I read, "The glory of the Chosen is based on humility; the life of penitence of Mary Magdalene earned her eternal joy. Through the ages her relics have attested to her spiritual presence in this site which has drawn to 'the sweet friend of Christ' multitudes in search of forgiveness and greater love." In the chapel dedicated to her, a prayer describes her as the patron of those imprisoned by demons. This intrigues me, for I feel I have been imprisoned by the demons of fear, pain, grief, shame, self-hate and sabotage for a long time.

Interestingly, the church and village are tourist attractions rather than places of prayer and pilgrimage. I have seen only one solitary figure praying in the crypt, and a couple in other places. While many candles are lit by the alcove dedicated to Mary Magdalene (and a few to Mary, the mother of Jesus), and the relics that attracted so many in past centuries still lie in the crypt and in the pillar by Mary Magdalene's statue, the place is devoid of prayer. Yet, there is something here. I sense it. A renaissance of vowed religious life has begun in this place, with the Jerusalem Community, a new group of monks and nuns from Paris, who have moved here. Like at Chartres, a holy spring, sought after and revered long before the Christian era, still flows.

I have chosen to spend three nights here because I need Vézelay's solitude, quiet and groundedness. There is no place to go, and only the birds and nature for entertainment. The scenery from the infirmary window is spectacular. The view over the rolling hills brings to mind Taizé, which is not too far away, as well as Cluny, two centres of renewal and revitalization for religious life. Something about the soil of France both resists vowed religious life and embraces it. I think about the people strolling through the church. Is it only history and architecture that draw them here at this time? Or does something of the majesty, awe and energy of this place of God open them to surprises, intuitions and hints of the Divine, even if they do not acknowledge this?

I spent the day in silent prayer in the crypt, cloister chapel and main church, around the ramparts of Vézelay, and in the spaces dedicated to Mary Magdalene and St. Thérèse of Lisieux, "The Little Flower." Statues and images of Thérèse, a Carmelite nun who died young and was later named a Doctor of the Church, are everywhere. Countless people still follow her "little way" to God, through ordinary acts of love and self-giving. She is ever present, in all the churches, always with fresh flowers blooming and candles burning brightly in front of her. I want to get to know her better.

Journal: Questions

I just came from a wonderful walk around the church. The gardens on the east side of the church overlook the valleys, farms and villages below. It is breathtakingly beautiful. Earlier I watched a video presentation on Vézelay in the church. It was fascinating, but have we forgotten the message behind the basilica and the incredible carvings that depict scenes from Scripture and antiquity etched over the doorways to the church? Are we in danger of losing the story that gives both meaning and unity to our lives as Christians? I hardly remember or even recognize some of the stories. For many in the West, our imagination and connectedness to Scripture have disappeared, and cool rationality and insight have taken over. This is tragic. When the churches such as Vézelay were built, the people who came there knew the stories of the Christian faith. Today, many do not. For inner transformation and healing to take place, our imagination needs to be stirred, engaged and urged to reflect upon God's saving love, compassion and forgiveness. The artwork and architecture provide the setting for our imaginations to flourish.

Meeting an American photographer

I started today feeling drained and very cold. In fact, the cool temperature in the twelfth-century infirmary/hotel left me with a chill and a bout of sneezing this morning. As the day wore on, I rested, had a relaxing lunch and then turned to intense prayer.

I began by focusing on opening myself to be embraced by Jesus' love for me and being willing to accept that love. At first, I felt only fear, distrust, shame, unworthiness, pain and grief. Yet, as the day unfolded, I found support for my quest in silent prayer before the Blessed Sacrament. I was drawn to the prayer there with the two members of the Jerusalem Community who sat there in silent prayer and openness to God. I felt I had come home and rediscovered a long-lost friend: comfort in the midst of toil and confusion. Even with the noise and the distractions of tour groups, something special was happening in the crypt where so many people have prayed over the centuries.

Going upstairs to the main church, I spent another half-hour in quiet prayer with the Jerusalem

Community, followed by Vespers. During Vespers, an American man I had seen praying earlier today leaned over and shared his book of psalms with me. I was happy to find a fellow traveller. During prayer and then Mass, I realized once again the power of a community gathered in prayer, receptive to God's voice and love and joined in the celebration of the Eucharist. The Jerusalem Community is a powerful symbol of unity, something I miss and hope to be part of at some point in my life. The symbol and ritual draw me in and tug at my imagination, pointing to a deeper reality in life and inviting each of us to pause and wonder what is at the core of our being as Christians and people of faith.

After Mass, I ate dinner with Neil, the American pilgrim. He explained that he was a university student who was doing a book on monasteries from a photographer's point of view. What intrigued me that most of his book will focus on new vowed religious communities that blend prayer, work and community life. Many of the members work part-time in the civic community so they can participate in the prayer of the group. He pointed out that the Jerusalem Community, which is less than 30 years old, already has three houses, with a fourth about to open, and there are more women members than men.

Our discussion focused upon monasteries and our desire for the sacred. In the new religious monastic groups he visited, all of French origin, he found prayer, peace and the presence of God, something he has not often sensed in the older forms of monasticism. He also mentioned that as in other walks of life, not everyone was happy, yet they come together in prayer throughout the day and pray for deliverance and God's mercy.

As we talked, I noted that many new forms of vowed religious life and religious movements have originated on French soil. Our conversation turned to Mary, the mother of God, who seems to be reverenced everywhere I go in France. He wondered at the connection: perhaps there are so many fresh movements in France because Mary, the mother of all disciples, occupies a special place in the hearts and minds of the French people.

Options and opportunities

Today has turned out to be full of twists and turns. First, I had lunch at the monastery. We talked about the vocation of being monastics in the heart of the city, of bringing prayer and spirituality to the people in their workplaces. Second, I realized that I had to trust in God's love for me and to say yes, God's love is enough, and that God will lead me where I need to go. Third, Neil, the photographer, suggested that I go and live with the Jerusalem Community in Paris for a week to get a better sense of the group. He then wanted me to collaborate with him on an article for the *New York Times* or a similar publication about the hunger for prayer, solitude and spirituality in today's culture. Finally, I agreed to forfeit the "official pilgrimage" and go where my heart leads me. I can't believe I am going to throw away all my other plans, but going back to Paris and visiting with the Jerusalem Community seems right. I am always interested in new movements, and here is my chance to experience a new movement in vowed religious life.

Lord, I don't know where all this is going, but I will trust in you – heart and soul. Tomorrow I will leave for Paris and spend several days there. This is turning out to be a real pilgrimage: I am being led by God to unexpected places, and my heart is being touched in ways I could never have imagined. And all this was sparked by some questions from a 24-year-old future medical student at Harvard who has taken two years off to do photography, pray and connect with monastic movements springing forth from the soil.

Part 3: Abbaye Notre Dame de Lerins, France

In a blaze of brilliant sunshine I arrived at this Cistercian monastery on an island in the Mediterranean Sea off the coast of Cannes, France. Why here? Partly, I am here on the recommendation of one of the members of the Jerusalem Community in Paris. There is incredible natural beauty on this small island. It's rather quiet, even though a lot of tourists seem to show up during the day to tour the environs, picnic on the shores and go swimming. But I guess my inner monk needs a lot of time around full-time monks. They renew my spirit. Although I am not called to the cloister and the silence/prayer/communal life they lead, I am still a monk.

When I look at where I have spent time over the years, a clear pattern starts to emerge: New Mallory in Iowa; the Camaldolese monks in Big Sur, California; Gethsemani in Kentucky; Taizé, France; the Trappists in Oregon and California. Now, on this trip, it's the Jerusalem Community in Vézelay and Paris, and the Cistercian monks here in Lerins, almost the cradle of monasticism in the West. I keep coming back to monasteries and being intrigued by them, fed by them and connected to them. In this way, I honour the inner monk and learn a new way of being in society. Some key words surface. Conserve energy – spiritual, psychological, emotional, etc. for the key things…don't get involved in everything. Find balance – what I do must be not only useful and helpful for the development of a more just society, but balanced, so that the inner monk is nurtured, protected and allowed to grow. The centre needs to be knowing, loving and serving God through prayer and work, in solitude and community.

The centre here is also silence. I need silence: not to balance things, but to listen. I have very little silence in my life. Partly, I have not wanted to be quiet. I have not wanted to hear the fear, shame, sorrow and grief stored there. I have fled silence for so long, but I cannot do it any longer. Nor can I deny the writer within me. I need to develop a way of life that

1. respects the silence,

2. honours the monk and writer seeking freedom,

3. accepts the wounds and allows for their trans-formation,

4. does work that is useful, gives glory to God and helps build the kingdom, and

5. respects the fact that I have a hard time taking my inner realities seriously, and will need help and a willingness to start over many, many times along the way.

Reflections on Lerins

Over the years, people have told me that I am a "feeler," according to the Myers-Briggs Personality Type Indicator. The persona I have adopted and honed is that of a thinker, yet I feel deeply and need to find creative and honest ways to express these feelings. Jacek, a monk with the Jerusalem Community in Paris, gave me an important insight: with the development of the artist comes a creative way to express feelings, emotions, dreams and desires. But it is also important to take good care of the body, exercising and eating properly. Clearly, I need to make some major changes. I fear that I will live these words if I do not: "The larger loneliness of our lives evolves from our unwillingness to spend ourselves, stir ourselves. We are always damping down our inner weather, permitting ourselves the comforts of postponement, of rehearsals."[12] This quote captures like nothing else what I have been living inside. I am lonely because I do not live/spend myself for my deepest passion. I have hooked onto a role and now the roles are collapsing around me. For instance, the vision and hopes that I once had for us Brothers of Holy Cross and the entire Congregation of Holy Cross in the Western world are finished, and I find myself wondering where it will all go. I am not sure there is a future for us collectively unless we make some major changes to how we focus our life, ministry and prayer. But change and redemption can occur; I need to allow my own change to take place, and others to change as well.

Also, I'm very upset about the recent changes to the way health care is delivered in Canada. The constant changing of roles, the regionalization of health-care services and the unknown future of Catholic/Christian health care have taken a huge toll on me. Fear has taken over, along with grief and sorrow. Part of the healing, I am sure, is to withdraw for a while, allow things to settle within and around me, and see how life unfolds. I need to move internally; for now, I will do what needs to be done. Otherwise, I am going to enjoy the summer, riding my bike, taking long walks, and finding the beauty of solitude and inner grieving.

The summons of the inner monk

It's already 9:30 p.m. and I have not written in my journal at all, but that's okay. Today was peaceful, and I am grateful for that. Tomorrow, I head back to Paris and then to London by train. I'm looking forward to the trip.

The breeze off the sea is wonderful! I woke up this morning feeling somewhat off-centre. I am not sure what that's all about, but I sense part of me does not want to leave the island. The solitude, quiet and beauty here heal me in ways that other places do not. Of course, I'm worried I will get into the same old ruts again when I go home, but I cannot allow that to happen. The messages have been very clear during my time here: write; trust in God's love, forgiveness and mercy; and move on. Now is a time to trust in ways that I have not done in the past, as well as a time to write and express my true voice.

The more I read about monastic spirituality, the more I feel called to give shape to it within my own life. What strikes me most is the willingness to be who you call me to be, Lord – to live from the heart and let go of the illusions, excuses and deceits I employ. Michael Casey, a Trappist monk in Australia, captures the focus for me:

The major concentration of monastic spirituality is in the area of man's becoming aware of his own interior dynamics; it aims to have man live from his personal centre, gradually becoming attuned to the inner promptings of grace and willing to cooperate with them. To find God, it is necessary to find one's heart.[13]

He goes on to say,

> The whole object of applying oneself to the reading of Scriptures (and other texts which mediate truth) is not to gather information, but to place oneself in a situation where one might hear the divine call and begin to put it into practice.... Lectio Divina is coming into contact with God's call at a particular time. It is directed toward self-knowledge.... The heart of "man"...is not found by introspective analysis, but by progressively learning to recognize the personal content of life.[14]

Yes, I think that is what has been happening to me. I have found a mirror of the life I would like to be leading – no, the life to which I am being called. It may not be the life of the monastery as such, but it's a life in which the monastic centre shapes my life, opens my heart, and frees me to follow with purity of heart and clarity of intention. I feel apprehensive about this task: I know how hard it is for me to live from the centre of my being, and how many times I have written that I would like to do so. Yet, there now exists an inner urgency to be one with life and to give my whole heart and soul over to it in a way that manifests God's love.

Everything I write and read reflects the heart's desire for authenticity, trust, creativity and openness. It's a movement away from the life I have constructed around illusions, control, distrust, defensiveness and fear towards one of love, trust, honesty, balance and attentiveness to the details of daily living, which take me either closer to or further away from God.

As I prepare to leave, my body is reacting to the upheaval. I am hot and sweaty, I have some diarrhea, and I think it is all about leaving. Am I going to honour my body? Am I going to listen and attend to it? Am I going to adopt a way of life that inwardly and outwardly respects who I am and who I am called to be? Those are the key questions. The answer is, I hope so. I have heard your voice call me loudly during my time in these monasteries. Their way of life mirrors the desire of my soul, and I cannot forget that. Now I must find a way of life that allows my true self to shine.

Some of the things I need to focus on:

- intentionality: know why I do what I do and whom I am serving;

- compunction: live with greater integrity;

- lectio divina: allow reading to shape my personal life;

- writing: let my soul release its insights and messages;

- solitude: find ways to honour that intrinsic need.

Lord, I will try with all my heart and soul, body and mind, to be more responsive to your call. Fill me with your loving grace and mercy, and may I co-operate with you and your grace at all times. Amen.

Later...

As the train moves towards Paris, I must admit that, deep down, I have not wanted to embrace who I am. Instead, I have wanted the best of all worlds while achieving very little of any. I am sure that the monk archetype has been pushing within me for years; I have just not wanted to claim it as mine. I have tried to be businessman, educator, single person, rich and poor, but the call clearly is to be a monk and to live that daily in all I do. I cannot move away from it any longer. I cannot deny it. I must shape my life accordingly. Being a monk is my way of being in the world and contributing to its sanctification and your glory. I will try not to abandon my heart, soul, body and mind again.

Part 4: Breakfast at the Penn Club, London

Cardiomimesis, according to Cistercian Michael Casey, "is the activity by which other objects mediate the self to the heart.... a person becomes aware of an aspect of truth of his being by recognizing himself reflected in the world around him."[15]

This morning, as I walked into the breakfast room of the Penn Club, a Quaker guesthouse in the heart of London, and looked around for a place to sit, I noticed a man sitting alone. After making sure the other seats at the table were free, I sat down.

As we chatted I learned that his name was David, he had just arrived by bus from the Western Hebrides, off the coast of Scotland, and he was on his way to a Quaker prayer meeting. He told me he had a degree in theology and philosophy, lived in a remote village of six houses, and made his living as an editor. The more I heard, the more I felt I was eating breakfast with someone deeply committed to living the Christian life. I asked him if he was a hermit. He replied, "Oh no. I see more people today than I did when I lived in London as a student!" Yet, I sensed within him the call of a hermit or mystic.

The more we talked, and the more I learned about his interests in the mystics and other spiritual writers, the more I experienced cardiomimesis. Something about his way of life, his dedication, his centredness and his openness to others, creation and God touched me and made me want to know more about him and how he lived his life. I read once that the essence of monastic spirituality shows itself in the quality of one's daily life lived in God's presence.

As I talked with David and a little later strolled with him through Russell Square, a beautiful park, I sensed that through him, I was seeing a picture of my own calling: a calling to a deeper centredness about who I am and how I live my life. I sensed, too, the call of the mystic, a call that fills me with fear. Maybe, like Thomas Merton,

I am finally coming out of a chrysalis. The years behind me seem strangely inert and negative, but I suppose that passivity was necessary. Now the pain and struggle of fighting my way out into something new and much bigger. I must see and embrace God in the whole world.[16]

While the time with David at the Penn Club at London was brief, the depth of it awakened my own potential and desire to greater integrity and wholeness.

Reflection Questions

1. How has chance revealed itself in my life?

2. What has happened to me because of chance encounters?

3. What possibilities have I missed because I ignored the wisdom to be gained from chance encounters?

4. Who are some of the people who have walked into my life unexpectedly and had a major impact upon me?

5. As I reflect upon my life, how do I see the hand of Providence in many of these chance encounters?

Food for Thought

We do not think ourselves into new ways of living. We live ourselves into new ways of thinking.— Richard Rohr

The dragon sits by the side of the road, watching those who pass. Beware lest he devour you. We go to the Father of Souls, but it is necessary to pass by the dragon.—St. Cyril of Jerusalem

4

Touching the Heights and Depths: Everest and the Spiritual Journey – A Conversation with David Rodney

I first met David Rodney when a mutual friend asked if Dave could rent some space in my apartment for a few months while he finished the course work for a master's degree in religious education at Newman Theological College in Edmonton. From that chance meeting, we became friends.

I once returned from a trip to Bangladesh dreadfully sick. I realized then that if I had not come home, I would have died. As time moved forward and the gravity of that situation deepened, my life changed and matured. With this experience of my close encounter with death in mind, I wondered how my friend Dave – a climber, presenter, writer and former high school religious studies teacher – fared on Mount Everest in the midst of punishing winds, blinding snow, stark fear and the ghosts of those buried along the trails.

Throughout history, the inner and outer journeys of others have fascinated us. Our imaginations are engaged by a person's trek to the North Pole, a friend's travels to a foreign land, or any story of a quest. Somewhere in the journey of the other we catch a glimmer of our own longing for adventure and the unknown. When the spark catches hold of a person to explore the outer realms of his or her life, the magic of the inner and outer journey combines to create the stuff of great drama.

The quest to climb Mount Everest has claimed the attention and lives of many. One of the remarkable aspects of the journey to Everest is the pushing of personal limits, both physical and spiritual. The climb to the heights takes place within the context of a living spirituality and a realization that the journey up and down is sacred. Many in the West may feel uncomfortable with the words and rituals of reverence and holiness, and yet the climb to the summit of Everest is a pilgrimage to a holy mountain; one does not return unchanged. As products of our Western culture, focused on speed, outcomes and achievements, we often lack the language or vocabulary for the movements and yearnings of our soul. Yet no one approaches the mysterious heights of Everest without awe, reverence and vulnerability.

The quest for the sacred is a universal experience. We long for connection, meaning and value in our lives. Over and over, geography has provided a window to the sacred. We seek out the experience of the holy through sound, nature, solitude and rituals. In doing so, awe, exuberance, peace and dread shape us. In these moments, the awe is not only a force felt out there, it stirs the depths of our being. We may not have the words for the feelings that envelop us, but we all sense them.

In Western society, the sense of the sacred has withered, while in more traditional societies, the ability to apprehend, value and hold the sacred in great awe and reverence is central. Indeed, many people feel that life is not worth living without this inner sense of the holy and the rituals that accompany it.

So why do we engage in quests that break new ground in our grasp of the sacred? The Buddha once said, "Existence has gone awry." Perhaps something has gone wrong or been altered in our lives – a divorce, a renewed love, the birth of a child, the death of a loved one, illness or a significant loss – and the opening within us leads to new adventures. For many, this something is the inner fragmentation of our present lives, or an undefined restlessness coupled with a desire for wholeness, that moves us onto a new path. We wish to feel truly alive in the depths of our being and connected to the deeper currents of life. In other words, the holy engulfs, surrounds and carries us into the deeper mysteries of life and gives substance and meaning to life. Substance and meaning do not always come easily, however.

Dave Rodney, from Calgary, Alberta, has reached the summit of Mount Everest twice in his life. While the journey to the top and back down are feats in themselves, the inner nature of the journey cannot be overlooked. What follows is an interview with Rodney concerning the inner significance of his climb, conducted a number of months after he first reached the summit of Everest.

Tom: David Douglas, in his book Wilderness Sojourn: Notes in the Desert Silence, *wrote, "The significance of the desert and mountain is not who resides here, but what we ourselves have left behind in coming."*[17] *What did you have to leave behind inwardly before you could move into the experience of the mountain?*

Dave: The conception of myself that I had let others build for me. For instance, my parents, my ex-wife, my employer and some of the people I thought were best friends had all led me to the belief that I was capable of accomplishing only so much…almost like a paint-by-number design of who I was. If I were to colour outside the borders, it was well beyond their realm of familiarity and comfort. What I really needed to do was to return to the beliefs that I had of myself as a child, when I really did believe anything is possible. And that the most important things in life are simple.

In my first Everest expedition, in which I was the communications coordinator, I discovered that with the right resources and attitudes and actions and personnel, if you have a dream, anything is possible, with the proviso that it is truly a call from something greater than yourself to move outside the box. What I learned was if I push my own thing, things do not happen. But if I step out of the way, and the right mix of people, attitudes and values emerge, anything has become possible.

Tom: After your first trip to the Everest area, you talked about the power of the Buddhist rituals surrounding the climb. The awe and reverence that the people native to the area hold for Everest is revealed in a deep spirituality. How does it show itself?

Dave: One thing I have to say is that Everest is not one of the more revered mountains in the Himalayas. There are many lower mountains and less auspicious peaks that are much more sacred to the Sherpa people. In fact, the most sacred mountains are in the lower valley where most of the people live.

The Sherpa people refer to Everest as *Chomolungma,* which means "mother goddess of the snows." They hold *Chomolungma* as sacred because she provides the water that sustains their life. That has nothing to do with it being the highest mountain in the world. It is the white person who has made it an object of conquest.

How the mountain experience shows its spirituality for me is in the Sherpa climbers, cooks and porters, and in the darkness, cold and wind, and expanse of everything from the Khumbu Icefall to the top of the world. In all my travels, I have never encountered a kinder, gentler or stronger group of people than the Sherpa. For instance, there are those who speak of "giving the shirt off their back." These people actually do it, and without any fanfare. Some of the Sherpa guides have climbed Everest five times before they are 30, yet they have no endorsements, sponsors or books to glorify or promote them. Climbing Everest is simply their job, and their rewards are of a totally different sort. The bottom line for me is that we have a lot to learn from them about ego, kindness, their relationship with nature and their spirituality, as well as about our relationship to the universe. For them it's not just about a Creator, it's about a universe charged with the presence of God. What I also learned from the Sherpas was that while Everest is a sacred place, the most sacred place is our own heart, mind, body and soul.

There is also the experience of the mountain. There is nothing quite like being halfway around the world and sleeping on an ice floe that is hundreds of feet thick, moving and cracking through the night. It strips you of all the masks and facades that you wear in front of family, friends and colleagues. Out there it's you and the mountain in an honesty that you just can't find in an urban jungle. You either have what it takes to survive, or the mountain will decide to eat you.

Above Camp Four, with only a third of the amount of oxygen we enjoy at sea level, reality somehow changes. As a result, our thought processes are significantly altered, if not diminished. At that time you enter an almost dreamlike state where you go back to the core of who you are. Your primal motivations cannot hide; you either manifest yourself as someone who will steal someone else's last breath of oxygen, or you will freely give of yours. All of your demons and guardian angels show themselves in a way that only those who have been up there can understand.

Tom: What is it about Everest and those types of climbs that propel many people to risk their lives and health?

Dave: There are as many reasons as there are climbers. But for me, it's about a life wish, not a death wish. St. Irenaeus said in the second century that "the glory of God is man fully alive." Nothing has changed since then. I have a need to experience life to the fullest, and so for me mountaineering is not so much about mountains as it is about the mental, physical, emotional, social, cultural and spiritual challenges I experience there.

I have also run into people who climb because of a need to fill a hole in their lives, whether it be a need to be recognized or anything else that compensates for wounds from childhood to the present.

Tom: St. Jerome wrote that "the desert strips us bare." From what I have read, the Everest journey does the same. How did this occur in your life?

Dave: That's a tough one! On Everest in 1997, I had a very quick phone call with my wife, from whom I was estranged. She said, "I have gone on with my life; you go on with your life. I have achieved closure with mine; now it's your turn." Here I was in one of the most remote regions of the world, and I felt stripped bare. Somehow I knew that this was for the best, and that my only true friends were myself, my Creator and the created world. I knew that there was a certain honesty in the relationship of the three that I did not have with the person who I thought I would be closest with at the time.

Within two years, I was given the opportunity to test who I really was and what my place was in the world by going back to Everest. The highest mountain in the world does not care whether you have a master's degree, are particularly religious, or are a good father. Everest is there, and how you behave under the harshest conditions that human beings can endure tells you everything you need to know about yourself. The only other thing I would say is that your integrity quotient cannot hide, just as the highest point on the planet cannot hide.

To quote Laurie Skreslet, "Mountains are the core of the earth exposed." They are there in full view; you can't help but admit they are there. Symbolically, you cannot deny your basest characteristics when you are struggling to survive. I came face to face with who I really am. That's appropriate: Everest is the closest we can come to God and still have our feet on the planet.

Tom: Mike Matthews, a 22-year-old climber from the UK, disappeared on the descent from the summit in the midst of a horrendous storm. What impact did his death have on you? What kind of questions does his death raise for you about the meaning of your life?

Dave: I think about Mike every day. In fact, I am still grieving his loss. We climbed together every day but summit day. Even on summit day, as I was descending the Hillary Step, and he was ascending, we had our last conversation. People say that there is a reason for everything, but Mike did not need to die. His death was avoidable. There were oxygen, communication and strategic problems – all human errors – that contributed to his death. At the same time, Mike's mountaineering inexperience and his drive to achieve may have complicated matters.

I sometimes wonder if part of the reason I survived was to tell his story. Mike was a young, energetic, charismatic and talented man. His life needs to live on in the hearts of those who loved him and in the minds of those he never met. But I hope others do not fall prey to such an unnecessary death caused by personal and professional ill judgment.

In terms of my own life, I have been asking myself, what am I truly called to do before my time on the planet is done? Is it to teach high school religious studies students, to speak about my Everest experiences, to write about the differences they have made in my life, to climb other mountains in the name of other awareness issues, or simply to climb the other mountains of my own life, such as dealing with issues of my family of origin and then, God willing, having a family of my own?

Tom: Carl Jung once said that "spirituality is the soul in search of its proper path." It seems to me that your spirituality is tied to this very image. Is what Jung says true for you? If so, how?

Dave: Every Everest climber is tempted with the possibility of becoming a media whore to sensationalize the sexiness of the mountain, which in this case is death. For me, the draw of this mountain or any other one is that it provides me with an environment that is conducive to enhancing my re-evaluation and re-prioritization of whatever it is I hold dear. It allows me the opportunity to re-energize, re-create and reinvigorate myself in a way that I have been unable to find anywhere else. For these reasons, I have named my company *Spiritquest*, because I ask this question: Are we in quest of the Spirit, or is the Spirit in quest of us? I am convinced that we are gifted with talents designated for a certain mission, and we owe it to ourselves and to God to determine what that is and live it out to the fullest. In fact, we simply must follow our soul as it seeks its proper path. In this way I am suggesting that Jung is exactly right.

Tom: In conclusion, what is the most important thing you have learned from your Everest experiences?

Dave: The discovery of who I am. I have learned that I am incredibly strong and capable of realities beyond any so-called realistic dreams. At the same time, I have learned that I am capable of unbelievable destruction of myself, my self-image and my relationships. I have also learned an honesty and patience with myself and my place in this world that goes far beyond all the books I have read, the degrees I have earned and the formal schooling I have been graced with.

This new self-knowledge is something I truly treasure and feel an obligation to share with others. More than anything, I trust that if there is fifteen minutes of fame associated with climbing Everest, people will get the message that it is crucial for them to discover who they truly are. The fortunate part is that they do not have to go to Everest to discover who they are. They might undergo such a process in everyday circumstances, whether that be a gruelling job situation or a tough day at home with the kids. Whatever circumstance provides them with, the undeniable test of learning their mission in life is a prize without price.

The great student of symbols, Mircea Eliade, wrote in his book *Patterns of Comparative Religion:* "The symbolic and religious significance of mountains is endless." He is correct. No one returns unchanged, and thankfully so.

Note: In 2001, Dave reached the summit of Mt. Everest again. He is the only Canadian to have done so. In 2004 he was elected to the Legislative Assembly in Alberta.

Reflection Questions

1. What elements of Dave Rodney's experience have also been mine?

2. Based on Carl Jung's statement that "spirituality is the soul in search of its proper path," how can my path best be described?

Food for Thought

Wrestling with God is of the essence of life.—Joan Chittister

No need to be afraid of fear, only afraid that fear will stop him or her from doing what's right. Courage means being well aware of the worst that can happen, being scared almost to death, and doing the right thing anyhow.—William Sloan Coffin

Pilgrims are poets who create by taking journeys.— Richard R. Niebuhr

5

Nudges of the Spirit

We are responsible for most of our own blindness and deafness. Yet the Spirit of God goes on renewing the gift.—John V. Taylor

The man who fears to be alone will never be anything but lonely, no matter how much he may surround himself with people. But the man who learns, in solitude and recollection, to be at peace with his own loneliness, and to prefer its reality to the illusion of merely natural companionship, comes to know the invisible companionship of God. Such a one is alone with God in all places. —Thomas Merton

On the day of Judgment God will only ask one question: Did you enjoy the world?—Traditional Jewish saying

Listening lies at the centre of the spiritual journey. St. Benedict opens his famous monastic Rule with the mandate "Listen." Listening means hearing more than words and sounds; it demands an inner attentiveness to sound, word, intuition, smell, gesture, dreams, comments and slips of the tongue. God speaks to us through all of these movements.

The American author Frederick Buechner once wrote, "If God speaks anywhere, it is into our personal lives that God speaks."[18] Listening also involves wrestling with God, as we know from the pleadings of the psalmist: "My God, my God, why have you forsaken me? Why are you so far from helping me, from the words of my groaning?... Do not be far from me, for trouble is near and there is no one to help." (Psalm 22:1, 11) Another example is that of Jesus' agony in the Garden of Gethsemane, as he sought to listen to the voice of God moving inside him. Listening to the nudges of God requires patience as well as a willingness to live with uncertainty and to test what we hear to make sure it flows from God and not our imagination.

Our inner life is rarely nurtured in today's society. Where do we go to learn how to pray, how to be attentive to the murmurings of the Spirit? Who are the masters who can lead us into the inner world? Where are the places that nurture the soul and invite us to pause and be still? Without this support, the person who hears the call of the pilgrim often finds himself or herself alone.

Nonetheless, the invitation to listen to God's nudgings deep within us moves us from a life tied to various obligations to a life of integrity – but only after we become willing to question, struggle with and shed many of the "shoulds" that have stopped being life-giving. As Thomas Merton said, "We make ourselves real by telling the truth."[19] In order to tell the truth, we must listen, understand and act. Transformation begins with listening and shows itself in action. Thus, wherever we find ourselves on the journey, the day is always new. We can listen to the dreams of the night, the intuitions of the day or the slips of the tongue that come from us or are directed at us, for all of these are ways in which God nudges us into a life of integrity.

Part 1: An Intuition on Friday the 13th

Over the last two decades, I have been intrigued by the renewal and rebirth of vowed religious life and spirituality within the Christian tradition. Why do some groups die, while others continue to regenerate? I have written a dissertation on this topic, given talks on it, written a few articles for publication, read books and articles about it, and visited communities that have emerged in recent years. Today I got up at 6:30 a.m., something I never do, when a powerful intuition hit me. It just would not let me go back to sleep or stay in bed any longer.

Last night, I was reading some theological reflections on the desert fathers and mothers in the early Christian tradition. The writer made the point that the spiritual renewal and transformation of people usually flowed from the experience of individuals who intentionally sought inner and outer solitude within the desert as well as gaining insight from the desert mothers and fathers. Strangely, a monk in a remote monastery I visited in Italy offered the same insight. "The renewal of society and people," he said, "always starts from within a person who has gone to the desert/monastery and flows outward." The book I was reading quoted a Jesuit priest named I. Hausheer, who said, "If you study the history of spirituality or the spiritual life of the Church, you will find that each time there is a spiritual renewal in the Church, the desert fathers are present." I find these insights fascinating and, at the same time, intimidating. The words of the Italian monk have stayed with me, and in fact still send a chill through me. Somehow they seem to apply to me. Intellectually, I am intrigued by this insight, for I would love to see a rebirth of vowed religious life in the West.

In a way, my calling feels very clear. God is asking me to be like the monk in the desert who opens himself to being changed by God. Simple? Not for me! It means letting go of always trying to control things – my destiny, my time or my engagements – which is something I strongly desire. More important, it involves moving from an intellectual way of seeing the renewal of vowed religious life into a practical way of soulful living. Even though I am not sure this is where I want to go, I feel summoned to change. That intuition is turning my life upside down right now.

As I begin the day, I am filled with questions as well as some apprehension about the future of my job and the type of contribution I can make to society at this time in my life. And yet, here on Friday the 13th, despite my anxiety and ambiguity, I feel an inner peace and wholeness that I have not felt for a long time. I must have touched a kernel of truth in the readings and in my intuitions. God seems to be asking me to trust unconditionally in God's Providence and in the words of Dame Julian of Norwich: "All shall be well, and all shall be well, and all manner of things shall

be well." Of course, having that level of trust is easier
said than done!

I am going to give life to my intuitions. What do I
have to lose? Thomas Merton, in a prayer/poem, iden-
tifies both my inner and outer pilgrimage, my struggles
and fears as I walk the path in front of me.

O Lord God,
I have no idea where I am going.
I do not see the road ahead of me.
I cannot know for certain where it will end.

Nor do I really know myself,
and the fact that I think
I am following Your will
does not mean that I am actually doing so.
But I believe
that the desire to please You
does in fact please You.
And I hope I have that desire
in all that I am doing.

I hope that I will never do anything
apart from that desire.
And I know that if I do this
You will lead me by the right road,
though I may know nothing about it.

Therefore I will trust You always
though I may seem to be lost
and in the shadow of death.
I will not fear,

for You are ever with me,
and You will never leave me
to face my perils alone.[20]

Clearly, I need to listen to and trust the voice of God in my life.

Part 2: The Isle of Iona, Scotland – A Sacred Place

The isle of Iona has been at the centre of my thoughts as I try to grapple with the intuition of the desert experience and the evolution of renewal of Christian organizations. Ever since I first heard about this place, I wanted to go there – not only to see it but to absorb some of its historical and religious energy. Part of me is very tactile and needs to be touching the actual location to get a sense of it. I guess I live up to my name. Just like the doubting Thomas in the Gospel, I need to see and touch.

Located off the west coast of Scotland, Iona is a small island about 5 kilometres long and 2.5 kilometres wide. Its Christian roots go back to the Irish monk Columba, who sailed to the island and established a small community in the Celtic monastic tradition there in 563. The monks initially lived in small huts scattered around a church in which they gathered for prayer. A group of monks later left Iona and established another monastery on the island of Lindisfarne, or "Holy Island." As with Mont Saint-Michel, Holy Island can be reached by land when the tides are low, but is cut off from the mainland during high tide.

The late Rev. George MacLeod, the founder of the modern Iona Community and rebuilder of the abbey church, is said to have described Iona as a "thin place…a place where the membrane between the material world and the world of spiritual realities is particularly thin."

The roots of Celtic spirituality

Celtic spirituality, like other approaches in the early Christian tradition, sought the desert experience as a place of renewal and transformation. While the Celts could not go to an actual desert, they could go to the sea. The sea and seafaring became their way of seeking God. In the Irish Celtic tradition, the ultimate point of spiritual wandering was what some writers describe as seeking the place of one's resurrection – living in the world as a stranger for Christ's sake. To the Irish Celtic monk who set out on the sea, the place of resurrection was the location appointed by God for that particular wanderer to settle and spend the remaining years of life doing penance and waiting for death.

For these monks, the seafaring life and the move to a distant place offered a way to move beyond clan and home and become totally dependent upon God's love and mercy. Monks went to sea with the blessings of their monasteries, to avoid political feuds, or in response to an inner urge. The seafarer monk experienced the struggles of the desert in the form of the unpredictable and rough elements of sea and wind.

Celtic monastic life survived in Iona from 563 until 1165. A Benedictine abbey of men was founded sometime after 1200, with the Benedictines absorbing some of the remnants of the Celtic community. The Benedictine monks built their buildings on the foundations of the Celtic structures and adjacent to Columba's shrine. Later, Benedictine nuns came and built a monastery as well.

Pilgrimages in the Celtic tradition were real tests of faith and commitment. People were asked to leave their family, homeland, friends and religious community. Some of the great wayfarers, such as Columbanus, preached the essential instability and transitory nature of life. Life for him and others became a perpetual journey. Religious pilgrims embraced spiritual poverty by leaving behind all they knew, making themselves displaced persons, and allowing God alone to become the alpha and omega of their lives.

Today, Iona welcomes pilgrims of all types. Tourist pilgrims arrive by boat, spend a few hours touring the abbey and the ruins of the nuns' convent, purchase a meal or souvenir and head back to the Isle of Mull or the city of Oban. Other pilgrims come to be part of the Iona community and stay a while. Various Christian traditions have set up retreat houses. Inns, bed and breakfasts and hotels are also available. But even though the accommodations have improved since the time of Columba, the journey to Iona is still an invitation to trust in God and be led where God wants us to go.

Journal: First impressions

I'm finally on the isle of Iona! The trip here was much longer than I expected: three hours north from Glasgow by train to Oban; a 45-minute ferry ride to Mull (in a raging rainstorm); an hour by bus across Mull on a one-lane highway; then ten minutes on a fiercely rocking ferry to Iona. Today has been wet and cold, but the rain is tapering off now. I thought it would be cooler, but it is quite pleasant here. Thank God!

I have spent the summer going back to the roots of different forms of vowed religious life as a means of better understanding the intuitions I have had and the things I have learned about the renewal of religious and spiritual life. The foundations of monastic life in Iona (St. Columba) and Lerins in the Mediterranean Sea (St. Honoré) both represent very early expressions of people seeking to say yes to God with all their hearts, minds, souls and bodies. The early monks here went out and lived the gospel through the quality of their lives and works.

Through the lives of these early monks and these historical and geographical connections to a particular place, something of the vitality of this way of life has endured, even though it has gone through various mutations. Although so much has changed since the sixth century, their lives and vision remain a felt presence on these islands, and a deep resonance dwells within many who come here. In both Iona and Lerins, I have felt the presence of the sacred.

As the bus worked its way across the island of Mull, I again felt the need for more solitude. Solitude is something I struggle with: I want it, yet I resist it when it appears.

My usual way of avoiding the call to solitude is to worry about what others think of my solitary behaviour in our very extroverted culture. I hear them whisper, "Doesn't he have anybody significant in his life to spend time with?" The perceived question and judgment eats away at me, pulling me away from solitude, creativity and self-exploration, and pushing me into frantic activity. No one has ever said any such thing to me directly; it's all part of my own insecurity.

I just walked through the abbey and the grounds here. I don't sense any life, vitality or holiness. Right now, it feels cold and empty. But then, so did Vézelay on my initial visit. Over the centuries, God has used this place to bring light and healing into the world. Although I seek solitude and quiet, those are very hard to find on this island that is filled with tourists.

It's about 6 p.m. now, and I have just finished a walk along the east coast of the island. The tourists have returned to the mainland, and the beauty and stillness are striking. I especially liked sitting in the ruins at the old nunnery not far from the harbour. It feels like sacred ground, and I am connected to the Spirit there. The abbey church leaves me feeling empty, bored and restless. I just can't sit there and pray — it feels so barren.

As I reflect upon the day, these themes surface:

1. God is preparing me for something, but I don't know what.

2. I need to write, but I am not sure what to write about or how to express myself.

3. I need to find, nurture and share my voice, trusting that through it God is choosing to live and work through me.

4. I am spiritually frail: not very holy; not very kind, caring or compassionate. I have a lot to learn.

5. I need to discover what is the best way for me to give shape to what is brewing inside me. How do I manifest my spirituality in the way I live my life?

I'll have to wait and see how these themes unfold.

* * *

The day is over now and I am tired. The prayer in the abbey with the group was good, as was the walk to the west end of the island. The sight of the sun covering the land this evening was breathtaking. Most of all, I am discovering you again, Jesus, and realizing that I need to find a way to give real blood and guts to the depth of your being in how I live my life. Following you is a new adventure for me. Allowing your mercy, kindness, gratitude, patience, compassion and protest to take shape within me is thrilling. But I must also say, Lord, I feel afraid. I realize to say yes to you is to say a firm no to my usual cynical, domineering, cutting way. I need to grow into this new way of being.

I really desire some soulmates. My recent trip to Notre Dame and the gathering of Holy Cross Brothers reminded me how important some of those guys are to me. After more than 30 years, they are part of me. I long for the comfort of deeper friendships at home and in my religious community. So, in the depth of my thanksgiving, I also hold some basic hopes and petitions.

The struggle to be patient

It was good to pray in the abbey church this morning, both alone and with the Iona community. I needed that sense of community. Lord, you provide what I need, but sometimes I don't know what I need. In many ways, since I left for graduate school I have had years of wandering in the desert. I continue to try to heal from the deep hurts and broken relationships, and at the same time find my true path. Now that I have re-established myself professionally, offered something of value and depth to the Canadian scene and reconnected to the Congregation of Holy Cross, part of that healing is complete.

Right now, I have no answers to these questions: What is my mission or call? How can I best live it, internally and externally? Iona is the perfect place to reflect, for from here groups in ancient and contemporary times have gone to live and preach the gospel. This summer of pilgrimage is about both discovering and strengthening my mission and vision.

I believe that the future has to do with living a more integrated spirituality, writing and being a spiritual director with individuals or groups. Furthermore, I sense that it demands that I stay with the process of refounding Christian health care and bring to it a faith-based position. But where does the inner monk fit into all this? I don't know.

As part of this commitment to a more integrated spirituality in thought, word and action, I need to bring renewed kindness, charity, compassion and integrity to my life. Right now I am resisting the commitment and the challenge of working with individuals and groups. I know I can't always have my way and be the great consultant, but I don't like the lack of star status!

Finding the 'missing piece'

For years, I have been searching for something. My friend Anthony likes to call it the "hidden or missing piece" that is blocked deep inside my soul. My life has been one of quiet desperation in which I have looked outside to fill the ache within. Nothing fills it. Numbed by pain, grief and isolation, I have created a persona of words, ideas and clever presentations, but the price has been a lingering loneliness. I need to keep in mind the insights of D.H. Lawrence in his poem "Healing":

I am not a mechanism, an assembly of various sections.
And it is not because the mechanism is working wrongly, that I am ill.
I am ill because of wounds to the soul, to the deep emotional self
and the wounds to the soul take a long, long time, only time can help
and patience, and a certain difficult repentance,
long, difficult repentance, realization of life's mistakes, and the freeing oneself
from the endless repetition of the mistake
which mankind at large has chosen to sanctify.

For me to write, I need to know my own voice, and that means writing from the heart.

The time in Iona revealed again my desire for stillness. Over the next few months, I need to find ways to embrace solitude, exercise regularly, be grateful for all that has come my way, and learn to savour the beautiful and good in myself, others and life.

People on Iona live in close relationship with the quiet of nature, the hidden beauty of birds and flowers, the ebb and flow of tides and rivers and human nature. I am too much of a consumer: I can see areas in which I can grow through observing the beauty that surrounds me.

In Iona, I enjoyed the solitude, the sights, the deepening realization that my heart seeks freedom, expression and recognition. My heart has been closed because of all the pain I carry. I have centred my life on work and performance. Now, I hope to live a more authentic journey that integrates body, mind and soul. Psychologist Marion Woodman wrote:

> Now that most people do not have a religious focus, the religious focus will go onto something else. They may think it's food they want, for example, because they experience themselves as starving. Well, the soul is starving; it's true, because it's not being recognized, and it's being continually starved.[21]

Part 3: Turkey – The Invitation to Surrender

The opportunity to go to Turkey emerged during my sabbatical time. I have friends there, and another friend who had business in London agreed to join me in Istanbul for a few days of joint adventure.

The roots of Eastern Christian spirituality and Christian orthodoxy are in Turkey, along with sites the Apostle Paul visited, including the supposed home of Mary, the mother of Jesus, outside Ephesus, and frescoed cave chapels and other places that have their origins in the Christian experience.

Initial impressions

I have been here in Istanbul for four days, but it feels longer. The location is spectacular. I have tasted all parts of my being: the longing for a deeper and richer life focused upon God, writing and teaching, as well as friendship. I cannot say enough about the beauty of this place and the people here.

The beauty

I feel a lot more peaceful than I have in the past, perhaps because I don't have to prove anything. I can relax and enjoy the goodness all around me. I needed a quiet day in a relaxing environment so I could come back to my centre and remember to be still.

Mosques and churches

As I walked into the mosques in Istanbul, the inner reality of *surrender* (the core of Islam) was all around me. Their sheer magnificence pulls me into a deeper sense of letting go. I have longed for surrender for years, but have resisted it. I fear it. But my dreams last night talked about endings and beginnings. The endings are about a life dominated by fear; the beginnings are about a renewed willingness to trust, love, and seek kindness and goodness.

A man preparing for prayer at the hamam (turkish bath) urged me to be centred and let myself go into the depths of my being. I heard him and I did not hear him, for he spoke the truth. When all is said and done, the theme is surrender to love, Providence and the eternal goodness dwelling in and around me.

The days have been very full. The walking, talking, driving and travelling have taken a great deal of energy, and there has not been much time to stop and reflect. I see why the Jesus Prayer (with the mantra "Lord Jesus Christ, have mercy upon me") is an integral part of Eastern Christian spirituality: it can bring you back to your centre in the midst of all kinds of noise and activity.

I have been dreaming a great deal lately. The academy where I first taught high school is back in my dreams again, and many of the dreams have me returning there at my present age. The days of teaching high school were a time of unprecedented growth and development, opportunity and insight for me. On all levels I was challenged to grow, change, adapt, respond and do what needed to be done. I played the redeemer/saviour/helper role to the hilt, and overperformed constantly. But I also struggled to find my voice, my limits, my spirit. Now it's time for a fresh start: a more balanced approach to life and service and a reconnection to the themes which first moved me.
Surrender!

Generosity and freedom

In the past week I travelled to Cappadocia and Ephesus, visited underground cities, spent time in ancient churches and mosques, and viewed some incredible scenery: towering caves on the hillsides; crater-like pockets in the terrain; pointed land designs filled with holes, caves and living spaces. But more important, this week was about the longing of my sensual/feeling side to be free, accepted and integrated into my life.

This longing has been pushing at my soul for as long as I can remember. My response has been to flee it, but I can flee no longer. In order to move beyond the frozen, underground and fragmented life I lead to a more holistic one, I must invite and nurture the daily opportunities I receive to live from my deepest and truest self.

Surrender has been a major theme again this week. Today at the mosque I felt the same need to surrender to the depth of the Divine Love living within and around me. The shift from fear to love is happening, but it will take time. A lot of images need to be shattered before the transformation will be complete.

The people of Turkey have taught me a great deal about kindness, hospitality, sensuality and generosity. They offer tea and conversation; they are willing to help. One person even wiped the sweat from my face. It has been a pleasure to be with them.

Concluding Thoughts

Listening demands that I surrender control. It makes me create a space deep inside me. For monks long ago, the cloister garden provided an open space for light, reflection and beauty. Often a fountain of running water marked the centre of the garden. I must create my own inner garden within the cloister of my life if I am going to listen to what is emerging and find the courage to act upon it. Renewal begins within me, but I cannot force it. The silent beauty of Iona, the hospitality of the Turkish people, and the aura of the mosques I visited reminds me that new life begins when we make room for it. The words of French theologian and writer Jean Danielou capture for me the essence of the journey ahead and the daily challenge it poses.

I have a need
of such a clearance
as the Saviour effected in the temple of Jerusalem
a riddance of the clutter
of what is secondary
that blocks the way
to the all-important central emptiness
which is filled
with the presence of God alone.[22]

Reflection Questions

1. What's the best way for me to listen to God's voice?

2. What or where are some of my favourite spots for connecting with God?

3. How do I discern God's voice in the midst of everything else?

Food for Thought

Do you really want to be converted? Are you willing to be transformed? Or do you keep clutching your old ways of life with one hand while with the other you beg people to help you change?... It is not a question of willpower. You have to trust the inner voice that shows the way. You know that inner voice. You turn to it often. But after you have heard with clarity what you are asked to do, you start raising questions, fabricating objections, and seeking everyone else's opinion. Thus you become entangled in countless often contradictory thoughts, feelings and ideas and lose touch with God in you.—Henri Nouwen

Do not seek to follow in the footsteps of the men of old. Seek what they sought.—Matsuo Basho

6

Parasites and Spirituality: A Sabbatical Journey to Bangladesh

In the body there is a little shrine.
In that shrine there is a lotus.
In that lotus there is a little space.
What is it that lives in that little space?
The whole universe is in that little space,
because the creator,
the source of it all,
is in the heart of each one of us.
—Parable from the *Upanishads*

Bangladesh, carved out of India on the eastern frontier of Bengal as East Pakistan at the time of partition, and part of Pakistan until independence was achieved in a bloody fight in 1971, has a special place in my heart. I first visited the Holy Cross community in Dhaka and elsewhere in 1986 to give a series of presentations on spirituality and the vowed Christian life. Over those five weeks, I visited the homes and villages of many of the Bangladeshi brothers. Over and over again, I was awed by the people's hospitality to me, a stranger. Even the poorest of the poor, whose homes were made of cow dung, offered me tea and rice and a welcoming smile. Their hospitality knew no bounds.

It was in Bangladesh, while I was sitting on a chair in someone's yard in a small village, resting, that I deeply sensed the unity of the universe. I was filled with a tremendous sense of wonder and wholeness. When I came out of my reverie, which lasted only a few seconds, I felt changed. I felt especially touched by God at that moment, and have carried a deep affinity for the people and life of Bangladesh within me ever since.

It was such an overwhelming experience, I couldn't talk about it; I did not have the words to communicate it. Only a couple of years later, during a course on Asian Christian spirituality, was I able to share the experience with someone. At one point I thought I was called to work as a teacher with the Holy Cross community in Bangladesh. Looking back, I realize that I wanted to recapture that moment of the sacred. I know now that those moments cannot be recaptured; we do better to savour them and allow them to nourish us for our ongoing journey.

My second trip to Bangladesh, to do research for my doctoral dissertation, ignited the same sense of wonder: I travelled by night train from Chittagong to Dhaka, watched the morning come alive at the Dhaka train station, celebrated Christmas Eve with fireworks and abundant food at all the houses in the village of Nagari, and spent Christmas day in Dhaka drinking "a thousand" cups of tea and tasting every type of pastry and sweet available. Everywhere, hospitality and an abiding sense of trust in God freed people to be themselves and enjoy life.

My third trip, however, took me by surprise.

This time I was on sabbatical. The first thing I noticed was the poor air quality. A black cloud hung over Dhaka the day I arrived. The road from the airport was filled, not with the ox carts of my first visit, but with motorized vehicles pumping exhaust into the air. Still, I was grateful to be back. I was looking forward to spending time with friends in the Dhaka and Chittagong area and then travelling on to Bangalore, India.

But before I knew it, I was feeling ill. I had never had trouble with the food or water before, but by the second day something deep inside of me had revolted.

I felt so awful, I thought I was dying. What follows is a reflection on what happened to me during and after that journey to Bangladesh. My illness and the six-month recovery period provided much food for thought.

Illness and Transformation: A Lesson Learned

When my seven-month sabbatical began on February 1, I was looking forward to an extended time of rest, reflection and renewal. Visiting friends in distant places and making time to read and write were other goals. After so many busy years, I needed to re-evaluate my life and let go of things that were no longer life-giving. Of course, I figured I could do all that in my head: I never expected parasites to show me the way.

Somewhere between medication and faith healing lie the healing and integration that lead to a balanced and holistic life. By befriending the parasites, learning their physical likes and dislikes, and exploring their symbolism, I opened myself up to a richer understanding of life and spirituality.

Despite feeling dead tired, four days into my sabbatical I flew from Edmonton, Alberta, via London to Dhaka, Bangladesh. I figured I would have no problems. I loved the food, the country and the way of life. What I did not love was Larium, the new anti-malaria drug I was taking.

Shortly after arriving in Dhaka, I took my weekly dose of Larium. Within hours, I was feeling miserable. At first I thought the nausea, lightheadedness and diarrhea were typical side-effects. I decided to go easy on the curry. As the day wore on, I was feeling worse and worse. By early evening, everything had lost all appeal. I tried to eat, and blamed the growing turmoil in my intestines on the anti-malaria pill. I wondered if I should keep taking it.

While Dhaka is malaria-free, people told me that the other places I would be going to were not. It was too risky not to take the pills. I did not like the options before me. Leaving Dhaka and heading into the northeast meant travelling by train, with squat toilets, to the India border, as well as walking a certain distance to the border crossing. Travelling through India with diarrhea meant asking the bus to stop so I could flee into the nearest ditch! My image of a sabbatical as a time of rest and renewal withered. Instead, I saw before me a nightmare of ditches, squat toilets and stomach cramps.

I remember lying on my bed in Dhaka sore and miserable and wondering about the sabbatical I had begun. I wrote in my journal:

> What do I need to be doing during this time alone? Being still is the theme that keeps emerging for me, and I need to consider it very carefully. How to do it? I have been looking for places to go, but the real place for me to go is inside. Like always, it takes something like the flu to turn me in the right direction. But what is the right direction? I sense that it flows from being at home within myself. I have spent so many of the last years fleeing myself; now I need to come home, be still, embrace all the parts of who I am and live accordingly.

Finally, I told my friends in Bangladesh that I was leaving. I could not do the trip and take the malaria pills. In order to get off the pills, I had to go home. I wrote an e-mail to other friends saying that for once I was going to listen to my body.

Getting out of Bangladesh requires patience. The morning I decided I had to get home as soon as possible, the country was in the midst of a nation-wide strike. Motorized transport was at a standstill, and most of the shops were closed. Via e-mail my travel agent said there were no seats available on British Airways for days. The strike was extended for another day, but on that third day my friend's travel agent found a seat for me on a Thai Airways flight to Bangkok and then on to London, where I could connect with a flight to

Edmonton. My journal captures my mood and thoughts on my last full day in Dhaka:

> Tomorrow, I head back to London via Bangkok and then off to Edmonton on Tuesday of next week. Thank God! Whereas at one time coming here was full of mystery and awe, now it's work...noisy, dirty, uncomfortable and dangerous. I see things now that I did not notice before. It's time to go home, sort all of this out and get on with my sabbatical.
>
> This experience reminds me that I am too hasty in making decisions. I don't take time to consider if they are the best ones for me at that time. I want to go home and be at home...that's my heart's desire right now.

Ironically, the day I left I felt somewhat better. Of course, there was nothing inside my stomach! In the early morning, as the motorized traffic returned to the streets and pushed the bicycle rickshaws to the side, I walked through the neighbourhood. I realized that this would probably be my last visit to Bangladesh.

I knew that the kind of travel I needed was an inner journey; I cannot look outside myself for other experiences or people to find the answers. I needed and desired to come to know the depth of my inner self in a way that I had never done before. I was being invited to touch, value and nurture the bright and warm hearth within me.

In London, another set of symptoms and concerns revealed themselves. There was blood in my stool and the diarrhea had returned with a vengeance. The blood was not a good sign, since I have been on blood thinners for years due to blood clots in one of my legs as a result of all the flying I did. I was worried; at the same time, I knew that something powerful and deep was happening, and I had to pay attention.

I had an inner dialogue to figure things out.

Me: So, what's going on?

Inner self: You are being cleaned out!

Me: I agree. But why now?

Inner self: It's the beginning of your sabbatical. It's time to change: to move in new directions, to look inside and not outside.

Me: I realize that. Does it take this amount of discomfort and unease to get the message across?

Inner self: Yes, it does. Otherwise you would be going in circles around Bangladesh and India, avoiding your life, your soul and your destiny.

Me: I agree with that, too.

Inner self: The trip clearly came out of a desire to fill gaps, not a soul-felt desire to be with friends.

Me: You're right. I went there out of a false sense of loyalty and responsibility…and to see how things have changed.

Inner self: I sensed that you were moving away from your true self. The only way I could get your attention was to work through your body. You listened, but there is a lot more to listen to yet. I want your attention, heart, mind and actions. I want you to become who God created you to be. For you to do that, you need to move beyond all your fears, self-distrust and disregard of your soul and move into love of your self and others. I know this is a tough message, but you don't listen unless I'm tough.

Me: True! So, what next?

Inner self: I want you to let go of all the junk…and there is a lot of junk accumulated within you. Think of what is going on as a good housecleaning. I am cleansing you of the fears that hold you back, the built-up resentment you carry, the insecurity that costs you so dearly.

Me: It has almost cost me my life. I have done a lot of things, seen a lot, but the hole at the centre of my being continues to yearn for something more, something different.

Inner self: Now is the time to go into your centre. Stop avoiding love, beauty and peace in your life. Let go of expectations, the images of life and service that are destroying you.

A week or so after leaving Edmonton, I was back again. I was very sick. I presumed I just had a bad case of diarrhea, even though all the anti-diarrhea medications I was taking were not working. When I saw my doctor, tests showed that my blood had become dangerously thin. Without immediate injections of Vitamin K, I might have bled to death. Other tests revealed parasites in my intestine, which I had probably picked up in Dhaka from drinking contaminated water.

What I had thought was a reaction to an anti-malaria pill saved my life. If I had not listened to my body, my return trip to Canada would have been in a wooden coffin.

As I look back, I see various themes emerging. While I knew when I headed off on my trip that I was dead tired, I pushed myself anyway. As everything started to unravel in Dhaka, I started to feel a persistent tug at the core of my being.

Back in Edmonton, the definition of a sabbatical as a time of rest re-emerged. When the parasites remained after the first doses of anti-parasite medication, I found myself living my sabbatical in a way I had not anticipated. Time appeared for reading and reflection. Solitude, which had eluded me for so long, became my companion, and I enjoyed it. The parasites were a constant reminder that healing was more than skin deep. At first, I wanted to treat them solely as a medical issue: give them the right medication and they will disappear, I believed.

After a few months of being on and off medication for these persistent visitors, I realized that I needed to view them symbolically.

Me: What is eating away at me?

Inner self: It's the drifting and not moving with those intuitions that feed your soul and give you genuine life. It's the need for an inner connectedness to your soul. It's the inaction that denies the mystery and dignity of your body, soul and mind. The mystery keeps opening to love and beauty and honours the deepest stillness within yourself and others.

Concluding Thoughts

Through the years, I have often defined spirituality as the glue that holds me together. Yet I still avoid and struggle with moving into the unknown and surrendering to the deeper mysteries of life.

Sabbatical for me was an intentional time to move deeper. While I had an agenda for it, the parasites revised that plan and pointed me towards the inner journey that begged for the time to mature. It often takes an internal assault on our bodies to grab our attention. In my case, the parasites slowed me down, led me into the depths of my soul, provided the solitude I needed and allowed me to wrestle with my demons in a way I could not have done otherwise.

Reflection Questions

1. What experiences have revealed God's voice in my life?
2. In what ways have I been asked to trust in God's Providence?
3. Which geographical places have awakened God's presence in my life?
4. In what ways has illness brought me to a deeper understanding of myself?
5. What moments of quiet awareness of God's presence in my life have I had? Who have I shared them with?

Food for Thought

God preserve us
from vision too explicit,
from compulsion to tell more
than can be understood.—Ruth Bidgood

Healing may not be so much about getting better
as about letting go of everything that isn't you – all
of the expectations, all of the beliefs – and becoming who you are. Not a better you, but a realer
you.—Rachel Remen, MD

If we are ever to understand the role of prayer in
healing and the relationship between spirituality
and health, we shall have to grow more tolerant of
ambiguity and mystery.—Larry Dossey, MD

7

Breaking Through the Numbness: Journal Entries Along the Way

O that today you would listen to his voice!
Do not harden your hearts, as at Meribah,
as on the day at Massah in the wilderness,
when your ancestors tested me, and put me
to the proof, though they had seen my work.
—Psalm 95:7-9

A new heart I will give you, and a new spirit I will
put within you; and I will remove from your body
the heart of stone and give you a heart of flesh. I
will put my spirit within you, and make you follow
my statutes and be careful to observe my ordinan-
ces.—Ezekiel 36:26-27

The nature of pilgrimage is to be touched by God and God's presence in the world. On this particular journey, I came to Ireland in search of holy places. I wanted the holy places to do something for me. I was hungry for something to shake off the lethargy I felt deep within my soul.

In the end, I did not visit many holy places. Instead, as I travelled around the country, I got in touch with some deep-seated numbness within me. At the same time, I felt the healing power of nature, friends and casual conversations.

Part I: Ireland

Journal: Touching the core

I am enjoying my visit here in Lisdoonvarna, but feel a numbness at my core. The stillness, the community connectedness and the beauty of this place all reveal to me that in my dash to work, perform and make work my main focus, I have missed the sheer joy and beauty of living. How do I break through the numbness? I need people to challenge me if I am going to find liberation and integration.

I pray that I can make the turn in the road you are asking of me, Lord. Until now, work has covered, fortified and defined my centre and hidden my true and noble self. It's time to discover who and what is at the core of my being.

A restless night

Yesterday I felt surprisingly at peace and one with the universe. After I arrived in Athlone, we drove immediately to the ruins of Clonmacnoise Abbey, which was started in the 600s on the river Shannon. Surviving in various forms for almost 600 more years, it lived different stages of monasticism and continues to draw people. Something very holy still permeates the place. And yet, when I went to bed I had trouble sleeping. I dreamed I was teaching high school again, but teaching subjects I was both academically and personally unprepared for. I think the dream was telling me I need to loosen up and work where I'm needed, not always be engaged in some super project to save the world. Work allows me to share my gifts and create a better world, but how can I best do that? As I listen to God's voice, I am hearing that change comes through love. How can I bring love, kindness, sacredness and integrity to all aspects of my life?

Looking at the elderly people today at Mass reminds me that I am aging, too. What do I want to be remembered for? I recall Columba's words that are inscribed on the bench in the ancient ruins of the nunnery in Iona: "Love is the only weapon that I have." Love – not cleverness, not power and prestige. For me, love continues to be the great abyss. It is a word I can hardly say, for it conjures up the pain, fear, aloneness and numbness that have characterized me. I just don't know how to express, acknowledge or honour it.

Lord, it is clear that you are walking this journey with me, and that I have a long way to go. Surrender, trust and love are feelings I too often push away. I fear that if I listen to them, I will end up going a very different way than what my ego has laid out. But it is time to listen to them.

On the road again

I am on the train to Dublin before heading off to Wales. I feel terrible, as if I have a huge hangover. Everything is pushing me inwards to question who I am, what I do, who I do it for. As I start to move out of the numbness, I might be surprised to discover that I don't always have to prove or defend myself. In the midst of this upheaval, I need to listen to you and your voice, Lord. The peacefulness of the last few days reminds me that there is more to me than building my identity around doing or proving that I have worth.

I have said it before, but I need to say it again to myself: I need to shed some extra pounds. I am getting heavier and heavier! I need to eat less, as an expression of love and care for myself. That way I can move beyond the numbness, self-sabotage and stuffing of feelings.

Part II: France

Honouring the sacred within

I woke up tired this morning. All night I tossed and turned on a bed that was too short. A layer of plastic under the bottom sheet made me hot and miserable.

While I had hoped to travel to Chartres Cathedral this morning, I quickly changed plans. I have been there many times before, but the bigger question is this: What am I looking for in Chartres that I cannot find in my own heart? All I need is within me. I just need to stop disturbing it with all my pet projects and escapades. This time is to help me step into places outside my ordinary environment where I can reflect, be more conscious of myself and who I am, discover God's call in my life and melt the numbness.

After trying to take a nap this morning, I finally got up, bought a newspaper and a cup of coffee, and went for a walk. As I strolled around my Parisian neighbourhood, I happened upon the Église Saint-Jacques du Haut-Pas, which has had a remarkable history as a hospital for pilgrims on the way to Compostella and as the parish church for many monasteries and convents. When I entered the church, I saw that Mass was being celebrated behind the main altar in a small open space. I walked to the side of the church and sat in an old choir stall.

Sitting there made me realize how interconnected people are. While the gathering around the altar revealed a mix of cultures and ages, it was also a reminder that, for almost a thousand years, people have gathered here to pray, to make themselves known to the Divine, despite revolutions and splinters in Church and society. In this and other ancient settings, God continually beckons to us.

God calls me to meet and liberate the Divine within me and not always to look outside for fulfillment. To be a bearer of the Divine means being aware of and honouring God's presence within me. I cannot continue to seek God in Chartres, at St. Joseph's Oratory in Montreal or on the isle of Iona if I am not first open to God's presence in me.

Knowing that others have touched and been touched by the Divine in these places gives comfort and hope on the journey. But I need first to summon the courage to meet God in the core of my being.

I knew there was a reason behind my poor sleep last night: it forced me to stay away from Chartres and turned me more towards my own story. By bringing me home to myself, it made me see that just as others struggled for decades to build the Chartres Cathedral, I have struggled for years to make room for the Divine within my own life story. The struggle continues, but I sense that an inner Chartres is taking form, and I need to be much more conscious in my building. I must also stop looking in the wrong places for God. Instead, I must start at home.

Inner monsters

As I sat in church today, I realized how much I operate out of a sense of scarcity rather than blessing or abundance. Because I focus on myself and what I need or desire, I find it hard to allow goodness and beauty to shape me.

My "inner monsters" are so powerful: they shrink the possibilities before me, drive me to perform well and seek admiration. They leave me little soul time, little personal time, and little knowledge of what I really want. I can hardly articulate what my soul needs.

In a group discussion I often see myself as a leper, as someone in great need of healing and change. Yet I am deeply afraid to share that with anyone, because it is contrary to the extroverted public persona I have developed over the years. I am afraid to be vulnerable, to show the sharp contrast between the public and private me.

Part of me wants friends, relationships, beauty and harmony in my life, but another part actively destroys all I seek in those areas. This poison eats away at me, causing much inner distress. I don't know how to make it through the inner wall that keeps me from connecting with others.

I feel that my true voice will not come forth unless I make friends with my inner monsters. Only then can I speak more authentically from within and take some risks with being vulnerable, intimate and tender with myself and with others.

Insights into voice

I just had a good visit with my friend Jacek, who is a member of the Jerusalem Community here in Paris. He gave me two important insights. First, the word "voice" in French – *voix* – is pronounced the same way as *voie*, or "way." I am looking for my voice/way in life. Second, he talked about Kathleen Norris's idea of celibacy as a place of hospitality to self, others and God, and about living that in an intentional way.

It hasn't been a place of hospitality for me. The choices I make from now on need to flow from a love for myself and the desire to be neither more nor less than I am called to be.

An inner dialogue

I awoke around 3:30 this morning thinking about my inner monsters. I sense they originally emerged to protect me from all the dangers and fears I experienced growing up, but now they are cutting me off from my true self and holding me back in relationships with myself, others and God. It is tempting to make some major external changes, but as a friend says, "Hell is portable." Leaving a job or other commitment will not free me from the monsters or automatically allow my true self/voice to emerge. At least, not yet. My present framework lets me search and discover my depths. I need to use this moment. It's as if there is a huge cement lid covering the core of my being: my task is to break through the lid and release the energy inside. The question is, how?

Inner self: The first step is to acknowledge that monsters are guarding it. Befriend them, and they may lift the lid. Articulate what you need.

Me: I need closer friends and a stronger sense of community.

Inner self: The inner place is the monk within. I know you hide and squirm, but it's your true and most authentic archetype. The reiki master you met at the guest house in Glastonbury was right: the monk is an enduring part of you. As you have looked for outer recognition, you have risked alienating and denying the monk who seeks to create an inner space of hospitality, gratitude, openness and gentleness towards your very self and the world around you. You do all kinds of things because others do them, because you are competitive, not because they complement your nature and give glory to God.

Me: Why?

Inner self: I guess that early on you realized that to get any attention, you needed to perform and perform well. Even as an adult you went back to being the scared and very lonely child, and performance at all costs became your way of being. You did good stuff, but now you need to find a balance. You need to nurture and care for yourself for the first time. You have feared your self, and the only way to keep the monsters at bay was to be so busy you could push them aside.

Meet the monsters. They are not cruel or heartless. In fact, they could be your friends and guides to the underworld of your hospitality, gratitude, tenderness and openness. They could be the answer to a prayer.

Others welcome you as a gift. You can do the same, if you drop the pretense and enjoy life more deeply.

Me: I have accumulated many hurts, rejections and misunderstandings that caused me much suffering. Part of me does not really trust in goodness, integrity, love and blessing. I don't even feel worthy of those things. The refrains of old still echo: "You are no good. If you don't shape up, we are going to send you away. You are a lazy, good-for-nothing bum. You are running away from life and responsibilities." All those destructive mantras. How do I move towards hospitality?

Inner self: First, take yourself seriously by deciding what you need for a balanced life. Not what you want, or what others have, but what you need. Second, keep praying for it. Third, take risks: seek to break through the resistance, the negative messages. Got it?

Me: Yes.

An invitation to be creative

It's cold and wet today. All I want to do is sleep. But the last line in a chapter of Kathleen Norris's book *The Cloister Walk*, which states that celibacy leads to hospitality, is on my mind: I have been "too full of stuff."

Hospitality: that is what is trying to emerge in my life. Hospitality to myself, to my needs, visions, hopes and dreams, and to all who come into my life. I fill up the inner space with so many projects, events, ruminations, that I am full instead of open. I enjoy teaching, but I'm too busy to create a space to be with the students. In my other work, which focuses on the awakening of Christian ministry, I lack space, energy and openness. I am stretched too far; there is no space for the outside commitments or the inner commitment to myself.

I am disgusted with my weight, which has a lot to do with hospitality, openness and love. I am afraid to deal with my strong emotions, urges, dreams and desires, so I stuff them down. I also stuff good and healthy feelings, because I don't know how to express them comfortably. Instead, I find it easier to eat my way through life, to avoid exercise, to hold onto tiredness, to show discomfort and anger rather than speaking or sharing my feelings in an appropriate manner.

Who or what is at the centre of my life? The question from *The Fisher King*, "Whom do you serve?" is key for me. I want to serve Jesus in all I do, but in reality, I serve the inner monsters of fear: fear of abandonment, failure, no recognition or admiration, job loss. I know that abundance, care and blessing come to me in numerous ways, but the defining emotion is fear. Now, my great fear is fear of illness. I wonder if holding onto so much junk within is causing my inner discomfort. I suspect that I'm not taking time to process things. I'm going too fast.

Inner self: It comes back to creating a hospitable place inside: a place for surprise, sorrow, happiness and so on. You are a sensitive person, not a machine.

Do something that takes commitment and frees your soul to be expressive. Find a nourishing way to be creative.

Part 3: Italy

I feel off balance: deceit, seduction, laziness and meanness are trying to guide me. This only prolongs my imprisonment in destructive patterns of relating to others and myself; it holds me hostage to broken-ness and destroys the goodness and grace trying to break through. It is good for me to be here in Assisi: the centre of peace and heart-filled expressions of loving-kindness. It is a supportive community, something I need for my spiritual growth. I need others around me who also sit and wait in front of the Lord. Yesterday there was nowhere to sit and be quiet. There was Mass, there was the tomb, and there were hordes of tourists. All the noise and activity just add to my restlessness and lingering meanness of spirit.

A person of integrity

Today is hot. I don't feel like doing much. However, I had an excellent private tour of the Basilica with Joseph Wood, a Franciscan brother. The Basilica and the paintings on its walls tell a wonderful story of healing, transformation and commitment, but what really touched me was Joe and his integrity. There was a wonderful energy about him as he told the story of the paintings and took me through parts of the monastery. He talked about time, and how much time it takes to do something well. I felt a stab of guilt as he spoke: although my time is consumed by activity, thinking, planning and reading, I don't take the time to explore an issue. I'd rather go from one thing to the next than master something in great depth.

Meeting someone like Brother Joseph reminds me how far I have to go to become centred, a person of depth and integrity. How much willpower, discernment and grace I need to blossom and grow into the person God invites me to be!

The gift of a prayer

The view is incredible from where I am staying: we are high over the valley, and when I sit on the patio, I can see forever.

It's been an unsettling day so far. The sky keeps changing, and I am feeling weary and frustrated. Part of me wants to go home. I can't put my finger on it, but I feel no spirit, no energy.

I need to turn and say yes in faith. Today I received a prayer from a nun behind the veiled cloister at the Church of St. Clare. She gave a copy to anyone who ventured to the back of the church, and she gave it to us in our native language. How did she know my mother tongue is English? The prayer is remarkably apt:

All-highest, glorious God,
cast your light into the darkness of my heart.
Give me right faith, firm hope
perfect charity and profound humility,
with wisdom and perception,
O Lord, so that I may do
what is truly your holy will.
Amen.

The prayer speaks to me of the heart of darkness, my closed-off heart. I resist, but the Lord keeps knocking. I will try to say yes. My future lies in my inner willingness to pay attention to the daily stuff of life as well as to create a centre of hospitality, kindness, gentleness, receptivity and gratitude.

The bottom line is that surrendering to God is hard work. Trust in Providence means overcoming long-standing patterns of alienation, hurt, resentment and displacement. Surrendering means opening my heart to what I desire most: love.

Part 4: Concluding Reflections

In our culture, we are not comfortable speaking of God. Instead, we focus on material objects, food and health. Being stuck or blocked spiritually numbs the heart to its true purpose in life, but at the same time offers us our greatest challenges and opportunities. The pilgrim tries to see past the daily concerns of life and listen deeply to God. We cannot move forward until we resolve to make concrete changes in the images of who we are and who we are invited to become.

The heart symbolizes our personal place of receptivity and response. The psalmist speaks of an open and listening heart when he prays, "My heart is ready, O God, my heart is ready" (Psalm 57:7). Are our hearts ready? Are we ready to be challenged by God's call and God's love? Are we willing to seek God's mercy and healing for our hurts, misunderstandings and resentment? Many of us may beg, "Create in me a clean heart, O God" (Psalm 51:10). We know our hearts are filled with noise and are not available to being opened, changed or moved in ways that our ego resists.

The words of the great German poet Rainer Rilke to a young writer give me hope that the answers and transformation will come. He writes,

Be patient toward all that is unsolved in your heart and...try to love the *questions themselves* liked locked rooms and like books that are written in a foreign language...live the questions now. Perhaps you will then gradually, without noticing it, live along some distant day into the answers.[23]

Reflection Questions

1. How does numbness of heart show itself in my life?

2. How do I grapple with it?

3. Michael Casey wrote, "The major concentration of monastic spirituality is in the area of a person's becoming aware of his or her own interior dynamics; it aims to have one live from his or her personal centre, gradually becoming attuned to the inner promptings of grace and willing to cooperate with them. To find God, it is necessary to find one's heart." How does this happen in my life?

4. How do I integrate my inner monk with my commitments and responsibilities?

5. What lessons from this chapter will I carry into my own life?

Food for Thought

An abba said, "The prophets wrote books, then came our fathers who put them into practice. Those who came after them learnt them by heart. Then came the present generation, who have written them out and put them into their window seats without using them."—The World of the Desert Fathers as quoted by Kathleen Norris

God wants the heart.—The Talmud

Sacred Places

Remove the sandals from your feet, for the place on which you are standing is holy ground. —Exodus 3:5

Martin in heaven here shines forth in the tomb— inscription on the tomb of St. Martin of Tours

A sacred place can be defined as such because it emanates an influence which goes beyond its physical form. It influences the psyche of man, his surroundings and sometimes even nature, as well as animals.—Sarah Ann Osmen

I was glad when they said to me,
"Let us go to the house of the Lord!"
Our feet are standing within your gates,
O Jerusalem.

Jerusalem – built as a city
that is bound firmly together.
To it the tribes go up,
the tribes of the Lord....

For the sake of my relatives and friends
I will say, "Peace be within you."
For the sake of the house of the Lord our God,

I will seek your good.
—Psalm 122:1-4, 8-9

Sacred places abound, depending upon who we are and what we value. A sacred place invites us to honour it and to allow it to speak to us. This may take time. We may awaken slowly to the message of the place, or it may burst forth right away.

Part 1: Cîteaux, France

A world of silence in which man keeps his word

You who enter these premises, remember that now, as for centuries past, you are entering a world of silence in which man keeps his word.

If you would heed their message, understand their history, unveil their mysterious secret, cease all idle talk and take your time.

Wood, stone, walls and land, the men gathered here within, invite you to set out on a journey to discover the best of yourself.

Have you ever taken the path where the world appears in all its pristine freshness, as pure and new as water gushing from its source? Have you ever thought that this source springs inexhaustible, joyous and fraternal from your innermost being?

For nine hundred years, Cîteaux and the entire Cistercian family have striven to illuminate the access to this source. As you walk around these grounds, listen with all your being to Him who has found you before even you seek Him: the Love which flows in you, infinite and eternally renewed. —F. Olivier Quenardel, Abbot of Cîteaux (posted in French, German, Spanish and English at the gates of the Abbey of Cîteaux)

The Abbaye Notre-Dame de Cîteaux – founded in 1098 by Robert of Molesme and nurtured and shaped by the life and writings of Bernard of Clairvaux, who joined the monks in Cîteaux in 1113 – is a 30-minute drive from Dijon. Like all monasteries, it provides a guesthouse for people seeking a time of retreat. The Abbey, which follows the Rule of St. Benedict that was crafted in the fifth century, stands as an enduring sign of God's presence in the world.

Over the years since the monks returned to Cîteaux in 1898 after being dispersed during the French Revolution, when their church was destroyed, the monastery has slowly come back to life. It was in 1898 that it was again proclaimed the motherhouse for the Cistercian Order.

As Timothy Radcliffe, a Dominican priest and best-selling author, said in a lecture to the Benedictine abbots in Rome in September 2000,

> I wish to claim that your monasteries disclose God not because of what you do or say, but perhaps because the monastic life has, at its centre, a space, a void in which God may show Himself. I wish to suggest that the rule of St. Benedict offers a sort of hollow centre to your lives, in which God may live and be glimpsed.[24]

Founded as a reform of the Benedictine Order, the Cistercians (sometimes known as the "white monks" because of the robes they wear) or Trappists (if they belong to that branch of the Cistercian family) are known for their commitment to community, prayer and work. For those on retreat at a Cistercian monastery, life centres around quiet prayer, communal meals, washing the dishes, setting the tables for the next meal, and creating a shared sense of community grounded in silence. The living conditions are spare, the wine, cheese and other food are outstanding and the monastic hospitality wonderful.

A rich variety of people moved through the mammoth guesthouse while I was there: a husband and wife with three of their teenage grandsons; an elderly couple; single and married people; priests; and others in search of a quiet place. Some people attended the church services; one spent his time drawing the rugged beauty of Cîteaux. One man who was about 30 spoke to me about his desire to become a monk of Cîteaux. Last year, he spent a week at the monastery; this year he will spend 30 days living with the monks as part of his discernment process. When I asked why he was considering the Cistercians and not some other group, he could only say he was drawn to the simplicity of their life, architecture and prayer. I was struck by the integrity of his words.

While so many vowed religious groups in the Catholic Church in the West lack new members, the monastery at Cîteaux has a few younger monks in addition to the observers like the man I talked to. Here in the desert of Cîteaux, the birthplace of the Cistercian order, a spiritual rebirth is underway.

Historically, the rebirth of the Christian experience in general and vowed religious life in particular has occurred in the wilderness and on the edges of society. I sense that it will be no different today. It's the lone person who finds his way to a place like Cîteaux and enters its silence and mystery and who in turn, through his witness and openness to the transforming presence of God, helps create the space for others to go deeper in their own lives. As a young monk enters the community, he sees the transforming power of those who have grown in the monastic lifestyle and been transformed. The path is not easy, but if the call is genuine, he can trust in the Providence of God to provide what he needs to be faithful to his calling. Life in the monastery, in the "desert," reminds us that God is ever present, ever waiting for us. We need only say yes to explore more fully the riches of life.

At the new church at Cîteaux, an example of contemporary Cistercian architecture that emphasizes the beauty of simple lines and all-white interiors, people are welcome to pray with the monks day and night. Throughout the day, people come to celebrate the Eucharist, chant the divine offices or sit in quiet prayer. The space encourages them to listen and be still. There, through the combined witness of the monks at prayer, one experiences the transforming power of God's action in a space made holy by prayer.

For those on retreat, the time apart is an opportunity to rethink priorities, let some things go and embrace other things. It's also a time to allow the silence to heal the broken and fragmented parts of our life. It's a time in which doing is replaced by being: being still, being present, and being stirred by a loving God who is always waiting and beckoning us deeper into the mystery of God's love and life. As the brochure distributed to visitors says,

> We offer a spiritual visit which leads right into the heart of monastic life. Everyone is invited to share the experience of the monks in the course of a journey which takes him through 900 years of history up to the time of the living community of today. Within the monastic enclosure, the person of today is offered an experience where the spiritual tradition puts him in touch with his own deepest questioning.

Journal: Quiet beauty

> It's so quiet here, it is almost scary. Why did I come here? I want to listen to the beauty of nature, listen to my Lord, and grow in wisdom and knowledge. Thomas Merton wrote, "It's essential to experience all the times and moods of one good place." On my next sabbatical, I will spend much of the time in Edmonton and let my soul, body and spirit grow there. That's what I need to do here. I need to sit with the beauty, let it speak to me and heal me.

Opening my heart

> My body does not know what to do when I have a chance to slow down and listen and be nurtured by the birds, trees and the glories of nature and solitude all around me.

I had a lot of time to read and reflect this morning. Again I hear you, Lord, calling me to make you the centre of my life. You have asked before and I have said "yes," but my "yes" demands action. My heart, not my head, needs to be engaged in the opening and discovery of your love and goodness within my life. My heart has been closed…locked away for a very long time. Now it wants to open again. Why is it taking me forever to say yes to you?

Hearing the call

As I sit and reflect, I realize over and over that I am called to be a Brother and a monk. I can best serve you by serving as a Brother, and need to trust that you will give me the graces I need to do this. Not only must my work reflect that inner call and commitment, but also every other aspect of my life. While it is easy for me to reflect on outer works, it is much harder to allow grace to work at the depths of my body, soul and mind where I have blocked, fled or feared it for so long.

I have been tied into a psycho-theology of self-help, trying to think my way through something and find a way to fix it instead of making room for grace. I have failed to find you in all things. I have written about grace, talked about it, and understood it intellectually, but I have doubted and resisted it. I know I have a lot to learn, but I sense I'm making progress.

Today is the feast of St. Benedict, patron of Europe, founder of the Benedictine order and author of its Rule. It's also my last day here. It has been very good to be in Cîteaux. Time here has allowed me to affirm the stirrings of my soul and my call to be a Brother/monk in all I do. If I can live my call with integrity and in co-operation with your grace, whatever I do will reflect your life within me. Yet as Bernard of Clairvaux and others have said, the hardest thing is to stay grounded in your love in the midst of daily living. I tend to compartmentalize my life; now I need to see all of life as holy and strive to live that way. I have been embarrassed and ashamed of my call. I have wanted to be something or someone I am not. At my very core, I am a Brother/monk, and my life needs to reflect that call in all the roles I play: consultant, teacher, friend, child of God. No longer can I deny or forget who I am called to be.

Part 2: Auschwitz-Birkenau, Poland

And the Lord said unto Cain:…
"The voice of thy brother's blood
crieth unto Me from the ground."
—Genesis 4:9-10 (quoted in the visitor's
guide)

What makes ground holy? Is it the blood of martyrs, the sense of the holy that permeates a place, or the perception and memory of the living? The death camps of Auschwitz-Birkenau meet all three requirements. Almost two million people were imprisoned, and most of them were killed, here under the cruelest of conditions during World War II. Today, from their blood, ashes and lived remembrance arises an experience of the sacred. This monument to death, evil and transformation points to the sacredness of all life. Within such holy spaces, the cries of our ancestors continue to be heard.

Holy ground. How many went to their death praying, "The Lord is my Shepherd, there is nothing I shall want. He leads me through a valley of darkness" (Psalm 23:1, 4)? How many cried out as Jesus did in the words of the psalmist, "My God, my God, why have your forsaken me?" (Psalm 22:1) As I walked through the barracks, the rooms of punishment, torture and death, as I stared uneasily at the mountains of collected human hair, shoes, toothbrushes, Jewish prayer shawls, artificial limbs, travel bags and baskets, children's toys and clothes, I heard the cries of the dead. I felt their suffering. Yes, this ground is holy. Flowers bloom and candles flicker in loving memory of those who were gassed, shot or starved to death.

Walking down the "dormitory" hallways, looking at photographs of the victims lining the walls, I suddenly recognized the family name of a friend from university. Jim, who had Polish roots, was born in a displaced persons' camp somewhere in Europe after the war. Was his family Jewish? Did they become Christian later? Or had this dead man been imprisoned for political reasons? Were other members of his family here? Did he pray? Where did he find God in the midst of this unbelievable suffering? Or did he cease to believe? He lived for a few months after coming to the camp. Did he know he was going to die, or did he hope he might live? Did he think about escaping or did he resign himself to his situation? How did he die?

A familiar name prompted a multitude of questions. Seeing a name I recognized made the experience personal. Riding back to Krakow in the train, I could not stop thinking about him.

In the last few years, the world has witnessed the killing fields of Rwanda, Sudan, Bosnia. How did we respond to these atrocities? How do we honour those who died because of their tribe, religious beliefs, sexual orientation or political leanings? Have we grown as a human family, or are we doomed to commit genocide over and over again? Did we learn anything from the horror of the Holocaust?

Holy ground can take many shapes. It affects each of us in a different way. We must not only remember but also recognize where violence, hatred and destruction find their way into our lives and the lives of those around us. If we ignore our own destructiveness and blindness, we too can kill.

As we walk through the "dormitories" of Auschwitz and the fields of Birkenau, and view the pond at Birkenau where the ashes of countless victims of the Holocaust were "buried," the voices of the dead will not let us forget that the road to true freedom, justice and love is a precarious one.

Part Three: Westminster Cathedral, London

> God is in his holy dwelling;
> He will give a home to the lonely,
> He gives power and strength to his people.
> —Psalm 68

Journal: Spiritual hunger

When I walked into the Roman Catholic Cathedral in Westminster today, Mass had just started. The words of Psalm 68, the entrance antiphon, fit the scene before me. The church was filled with a cross-section of humanity that represented a range of ages and ethnic origins. Heads bowed, people walked and prayed as they moved towards the communion table. At side altars, people lit candles as a way to break through their personal darkness. At the back of the church, penitents waited in line to confess their sins and receive forgiveness, while in another area, people sat in silent prayer before the Blessed Sacrament.

Throughout the day, numerous Masses are celebrated, scriptures read, prayers offered and sins forgiven. In the short time I was there, a Mass started at the main altar shortly after the one I attended finished. What struck me was the intense devotion of the people. In this age of spiritual hunger, the people gathered found a place of solace and comfort in God's dwelling. Our world is a noisy place, but a sense of stillness and the sacred permeated the building, and the psalmist's words, "God gives power and strength to his people," filled the cathedral. A sense of communion clearly existed between the people and their God.

Spending time at the cathedral reminded me of the power of certain places to quicken the soul and feed our spiritual hunger. In an era of closed or locked churches, where can we go to pray quietly and connect to the sacred? While we can stop and be quiet anywhere, sometimes it's important for the soul to be connected to the stories, images, symbols and spaces that remind us that God dwells in our midst. It's also good to be quiet with other seekers in search of God's strength and power. We tend to forget the power of a group gathered in silent prayer.

I taught courses on spirituality for a number of years. Time and time again I saw proof of the power of communal prayer to heal, bind and strengthen individuals and groups. I always reserved the last fifteen minutes of the three-hour class for quiet prayer. As the semester progressed, this came to be sacred time. If I had to shorten it for some reason, people complained. For many, this was their first taste of a group gathered in silence in the presence of God. For some, it was the only quiet time in their busy week.

Westminster Cathedral stands with its doors open as a place to nurture the soul. While tourists move quietly through the church, looking at its art and architecture, the overwhelming experience is of quiet prayer: prayer that reaches to the depth of the soul and to the heart of the Divine. This prayer is marked by participation in the Eucharist, sharing in the body and blood of Christ; by a pause at the tomb of the late Cardinal Hume; by a quiet prayer and candle lit in front of the medieval statue of Mary. In this place, our spiritual hunger can be satisfied, even for a moment, and our being strengthened for the day's journey.

Part 4: Czestochowa, Poland

Journal: Disorientation

My guidebook calls Czestochowa the Catholic Mecca of Poland. Our Lady of Czestochowa is important to the life and history of Poland; she is its patron and its protectress from invaders. This is very holy ground for many people.

Pilgrimage can be disorienting, as I was reminded today. My travelling companion and I arrived here by train from Krakow. We do not speak Polish and therefore could not understand the directions, find the tickets, or get our money changed without agonizing waits and paperwork. We walked and walked, and it was disorienting. The only familiar thing was McDonald's. It seems to be the place to eat in town, which is disappointing, but at least I could understand the menu.

Today was a frustrating day, and reminded me how impatient I can be. As I moved among the crowds in the chapel of the Black Madonna and church, where people were kneeling and praying all over the place, I wondered what was happening during the services. I found myself thinking, what is the great attraction here?

* * *

Today is better than yesterday. I found my glasses, which I had misplaced, and had some quiet time in the church between services. Although this place is a mystery to me, it certainly speaks to many: the depth of their prayer and piety is everywhere. Hushed silence fills the chapel where the icon of Mary is displayed. Quiet whispers of heartfelt prayers echo. People hide behind pillars and along the walls in silent attentiveness.

For these people, this shrine is holy ground and touches some primal spiritual energy. Something here triggers the pilgrims' imagination and moves their hearts. I can see people of all ages and stages here: young and old, mothers and fathers, children and grandparents, families and individuals. There are many groups of young people, adults, nuns, brothers and priests.

Unlike other places of popular Marian devotion, such as Lourdes, Knock (in Ireland) and Fatima, Czestochowa is thankfully devoid of the ubiquitous vendors of T-shirts, miniature replicas of the shrine and Mary, and other souvenirs. There are a few designated places where people can buy images and rosaries, but it's not intrusive. Groups are talking, walking, eating lunch, praying and enjoying one another's company, the park-like surroundings and the experience.

At this moment, this pilgrimage site and the icon of Mary are mystery to me. I will wait and see what emerges for me from this visit.

Part 5: St. Joseph's Oratory, Montreal

"If the work is from God, it will continue; if not, it will crumble," remarked Paul Bruchesi, Archbishop of Montreal, of the vision and work of Brother André, founder of St. Joseph's Oratory.

The work has not crumbled; it has only grown. On this beautiful spring morning in Montreal, busloads of pilgrims, schoolchildren and adults – people of all ages and nationalities – gather at the Oratory, atop Mount Royal. Some touch the feet of Jesus on the life-size crucifix in the crypt. Others light candles in front of statues dedicated to St. Joseph. Many file slowly past the tomb of Brother André, stopping to touch the tomb and say a prayer. Today, bouquets of fresh flowers are strewn across the tomb.

In the corridor leading to the promenade dedicated to St. Joseph, tucked into the wall on a small niche rests a small statue of Joseph holding Jesus. What is unusual

140

here is that both Joseph and Jesus wear crowns, and heated oil rests in front of the statue. St. Joseph's oil, which Brother André used to rub on the bodies of the sick, is said to have cured and healed many. (Part of the discomfort with Brother André during his lifetime, especially from the medical community, stemmed from his use of this oil.) Oil from this font in front of the statue of Joseph and Jesus continues to be sold at the Oratory. On either side of the statue are boxes. Pilgrims are invited to write down their prayer intentions on special pieces of paper, along with their home address, if they wish.

Throughout the Oratory, collections of crutches and plaques thank St. Joseph and Brother André for graces and favours received. The sick have always found a place of comfort and healing here. On Wednesday afternoons a special service is held for them. But it's not only those with physical ailments who come to pray. Others come, too. What continues to draw people to the Oratory today?

Reason provides no guide here. I believe that people sense the presence of the sacred on this mountaintop. Brother André certainly did. In his porter's room at Notre Dame College, André had a small statue of St. Joseph on his windowsill overlooking Mount Royal. When asked why Joseph's back was to him, he is said to have replied, "Because someday, St. Joseph is going to be honoured in a very special way on Mount Royal!" In time André's plan came to fruition. Patiently he waited for the money, energy, permission and acceptance to create a space for prayer and healing dedicated to St. Joseph, patron of Canada and the Catholic Church.

From André's actions, we learn much about his spirituality. His prayer, simple but direct, must have opened his heart to hear God's voice and to trust it, even when people vigorously attacked, misunderstood and denounced him as a charlatan. André's trust in God's enduring love for him and his mission guided him through periods of darkness and questioning. A simple lesson emerges for me: much of the spiritual journey is about waiting, trusting and hoping that an invisible God will continually guide, direct, and transform us and our lives.

Large numbers of people gather for Mass throughout the day and wander throughout the Oratory and the grounds. Many pilgrims light votive candles at shrines dedicated to St. Joseph, patron of the sick and of those struggling with evil spirits. Like people throughout history, we struggle often with our own inner demons – the unnameable and unpleasant parts of ourselves. The Bible reminds us that part of the Christian journey is not only recognizing these spirits and their power in our lives, but admitting that we need help during times of discouragement, entanglement and drivenness.

We cannot heal our shadow side only through a self-help book or a small group. Part of the transformation process is making peace with who we are and learning to accept God's forgiveness. As Brother André listened to people's stories, he discovered that often the healing they sought was not physical, but emotional or spiritual. Like them and like his patron, St. Joseph, André knew the demons of darkness, uncertainty, fear, temptation and brokenness.

As I watched people approach the crucifix near the front of the crypt to touch, hold or embrace the feet or ankles of Jesus, I realized how much we long to touch and be touched by the Divine.

Reflection Questions

1. Where are the sacred places in my life?
2. What and where are the sacred places in my religious and cultural history?
3. How does the sacred reveal itself to me in these places?
4. From my experience, what does a sacred place feel or smell like?
5. What touched me the most in this section? Why?

Food for Thought

If there is a trick to soulful travel, it is learning to see for yourself. To do this takes practice and a belief that it matters.—Phil Cousineau

If we lose and do not develop soul connections with people or lose touch with soul-renewing places or activities, we will gradually find that we are inhabiting our own wasteland.—Jean Shinoda Bolen

Life Lessons

Change means movement. Movement means
friction.—Saul Alinsky

Stand at the crossroads, and look,
and ask for the ancient paths,
where the good way lies;
and walk in it,
and find rest for your souls.
—Jeremiah 6:16

There is the other universe,
of the heart of man
That we know nothing of,
that we dare not explore.
....

Fore-runners have barely landed on the shore
And no man knows, no woman knows
The mystery of the interior
When darker still than Congo or Amazon
Flow the heart's rivers of fullness, desire and
distress.
—D.H. Lawrence

Life is a series of lessons, some of them obvious,
some of them not.—Joan Chittister

B eing a pilgrim continually brings us into contact
with people, places and events. Sometimes we
understand them; sometimes our imaginations and
minds are stretched; sometimes we pull back in revul-
sion or fear. None of us lives a life of perfect openness

and acceptance. We bring our personal and collective histories and filters to each experience.

Most of us learn best through experience. I can collect many ideas, but it is in daily living and my encounters with others and the world around me that I discover who I am.

Discernment – the ability to sift through the events of life – is the process we use to evaluate a situation. Discernment gives us a choice. Will we grapple with an issue or resist it with all our might? Sometimes the answer is obvious; sometimes it takes years of rumination before the meaning comes clear. Some questions remain with us until we die.

Walking the inner and outer pathways of pilgrimage provides endless opportunities for questions, defining experiences and candid observations. Discerning God's presence and voice is an ongoing process of stepping back, reflecting, listening and integrating what comes our way.

Part 1: Who Are the Poor? (Lourdes, France)

I am in Lourdes, in southwest France, on the edge of the foothills of the Pyrenees, for my third visit. This place is renowned for its healing powers for body, mind and spirit. According to the story, on February 11, 1858, in the grotto of Massabielle, near Lourdes, Mary, the mother of Jesus, appeared eighteen times to Bernadette Soubirous, a young peasant girl. Mary revealed herself to Bernadette as the Immaculate Conception, and asked that a chapel be built on the site of the vision. She told Bernadette to drink from a fountain in the grotto. Bernadette dug into the ground where Mary told her to dig, and a spring began to flow. The water from this spring has shown remarkable healing and transformative properties ever since.

The city sidewalks are unfortunately filled with gaudy souvenir shops selling items ranging from bottles for collecting water from the spring, to candles of every size, up to six feet tall, to tacky statues of Mary. I was happy to get through the gates of the shrine and into the sacred space of Lourdes. As usual, pilgrims were milling around in small and large groups. Some were heading directly to the grotto to touch the stone where Mary appeared to Bernadette and the healing water flows. Others filled their bottles with spring water from faucets protruding from a wall. Still others moved in and out of the various churches scattered around the area.

As people gathered in the evening for the candle-light procession from the grotto to the front of the main church, I was in awe of the assembled group. They came on foot, in wheelchairs, on hospital beds and stretchers accompanied by their nurses, friends, volunteers and family members. They came from nearby hotels and hospitals on the grounds. While the desire for physical healing no doubt brought many here, I am sure many more of us were there to pray for inner healing. Lourdes reminds us that no human being is fully whole; here, in our brokenness, we can all be one.

As I strolled though the gates into Lourdes, I was touched by the stillness and sense of the sacred that pervades it. Something very holy and alive dwells here. Pilgrims come from all over the world to touch the place where Mary stood, to collect the healing waters from the spring, to light a candle, to bathe in the waters of Lourdes in the area set aside for immersion, and to pray for healing. A student of mine in Edmonton used to visit a resident at a local nursing home. This woman, who had been to Lourdes, explained that the experience "was not a curing of my body but a healing of my soul. I am now at peace and ready to move into the next stage of my life."

What does a place like this teach me? I learn humility and stand stark naked before God. I am drawn here by the tangible feeling of God's presence, the strength of people at prayer and the desire to be part of the energy of the prayer.

Lourdes paints an amazing picture of humanity in search of the Divine. Outside the walls, as in any pilgrim community, entrepreneurs seek to provide pilgrims not only with food and shelter, but other necessary items as well. They also sell souvenirs: bottles for water; candles; medals; rosaries; holy water fonts; images, statues and icons of Mary, Jesus and the saints; books, cards and crafts. At the gates, the poor are begging, yet inside the gates, we are all poor before God. We all seek healing for the broken, unhealthy, or fragmented parts of our lives so we can again touch the depth of God's wholeness and holiness within us and in the world around us.

Part 2: Wrestling with the Demons (St. Raphael and Frankfurt)

As we pulled into the station at St. Raphael, France, a man about 30 years old threw himself at the train. The loudspeaker announced that there had been an accident. I walked to the next car; there on the ground, covered in blood, lay the twisted body. Rescue squads from the fire department quickly turned him over, administered oxygen and started pumping his chest. Gradually, life started to return. When the ambulance crew arrived, they checked his wounds, took his blood pressure and hooked him up to a monitor to watch his heartbeat. On the train, some people watched, while others looked away. On the platform, most turned away and waited for the scene to change.

Out of the crowd, an elegantly dressed woman quickly approached the man, asked for some gloves and started to help. When the paramedic could not find a vein to collect some blood and start an intravenous line, she found a vein in the other arm, took blood, got the IV started and helped lift the injured man onto a stretcher, across the tracks and into a waiting ambulance. The crisis was over. The blood was washed off the platform, the bandages were picked up and we continued on our journey.

In Frankfurt, Germany, hunched by the wall, a disheveled man shoved a needle into his arm. A little farther away, I noticed a group of three intently preparing to inject themselves with heroin. Hordes of people passed by, ignoring and avoiding them.

A little later, I saw a couple of policemen patrolling the street. Nonchalantly, they walked by the ragged-looking man and a woman feeding their heroin habit. No one responded.

Why do we fall so easily into self-destructive patterns? What are the demons that eat away at our souls, paralyze us with fear and inflict pain, despair and darkness onto our bodies, minds and souls? The desert mothers and fathers of the early Church often talked about their movement to the desert as a time to "wrestle with the demons." We know from the book of Genesis that Jacob wrestled with the angel through the night and prevailed. Yet even he limped away, full of the effects of the experience.

We all know what our own demons are. Why do some of us wrestle with them and break free, while others block them out, feel powerless before them and blindly obey them? Why do some fall prey to them and are ruled unto death by them? Part of our spiritual journey is to wrestle with the demons, but in the context of God's love and grace. If life has become so desolate and no signs of hope or love remain, the promise of drugs and other addictions is to ease the pain, at least for a while. In our demons lies our pain.

A number of years ago, when I was studying spiritual direction, one of the teachers reminded us that as humans we are capable of terrible atrocities. As spiritual directors, he said, we would discover within us powers of self-destruction, hate, greed, jealousy, fear and rage. He warned us not to underestimate our own powers of evil and destruction, and not to forget that these tendencies live in us. The challenge, he said, was to accept these realities so we could be compassionate to ourselves and to others. If we didn't accept them, he warned, they would rule us and we would focus on judging others.

A pilgrim I once met said we are all "houses of God." He's right. But do we know it? How do we care for our house? How do we care for the houses of others? In many parts of our lives, our spirits call out for attention, nourishment and dialogue. I need to keep asking myself, am I willing to wrestle with my demons? Am I open to being healed? Do I like my demons too much to want to change? Or am I like the people shoving needles into their arms? Am I like the man trying to self-destruct?

For the desert writers, wrestling with our demons leads to compassion and an awareness of how God's grace works in our lives. In the struggle, we discover our openness to co-operating with grace and welcome God into our lives.

Being on pilgrimage is about noticing what happens outside and inside us. The tragedy outside reminds us that we, too, can self-destruct if we don't wrestle with our demons and seek ways to co-operate with God's grace.

Part 3: Hungry but Not Fed (London)

I went out walking in London this afternoon with no clear destination. As I walked through Covent Garden and through Drury Lane, I realized that St. Paul's Cathedral could not be far away. Seeing the impressive dome, I made my way to the church. When I got there, Evensong had begun. I found a seat and sat down.

As the service unfolded, I found myself growing more and more restless. While the music was beautiful, I could not participate. The choir and action were so distant from the people! It felt like I was at a performance, not joining in communal prayer. Some people left partway through the service; perhaps they had another appointment, or maybe the service was not touching their need.

I found myself looking forward to the sermon. There, I figured, I would find nourishment. Instead, I heard a lecture on church history. Like so many other times, I went into church hungry and came out starving. I had hoped to be fed by the music, the majesty of the edifice, the readings, prayers and sermon. Instead, I was left wondering how this service related to me and the world around me. How long can the Church continue to be remote and formal when so many crave being touched by the Divine and helped through ritual, song and word to name their religious experiences and give shape to their prayers?

Part 4: Waiting (Czestochowa)

All we want to do is change some money. We walk into a bank and a man says, "Go to Booth 1." We go. We wait and wait and wait. First the line is slow, and then it stops. The people in the next line are moving, doing their business and moving on. Our line is still stopped. People start to get restless. Some sit. Some complain out loud. I tap my hand on the counter, shift from one foot to the other, then lean against the counter. Still nothing happens. Forty-five minutes pass. It's hot. People groan. The man at the wicket does not look back. The teller behind the glass wall looks nervous. Still no movement.

Then, he's done. On his way out he says, in English, "It's not my fault." I want to yell, Whose fault is it? The woman in front of me quickly changes her Belgian francs into the local currency. Then it's my turn. I show the teller my traveller's cheques and she says, "No!" I think I'm going to pass out from frustration and rage. I pull some deutschmarks out of my pocket and shove them under the glass. She takes them and changes them into Polish currency. Then she calls someone who brings my friend and me to another desk. More papers to fill out. Three forms in all must be marked in different ways and with different data. We wait some more. She goes away. We wait. Finally, she comes back with more paper. But tucked inside the paper is the money. We sign and leave. Great, we say, now all we have to do is pick up our train tickets.

We get there. There are lineups. Please sit, they say. We sit. How long will it take to do the ticket? we ask. Oh, about 60 minutes. They have no computers and will have to telephone for the various seats and locations. What have we gotten ourselves into? Enough! We will come back later. Can you have it ready by 5:00 p.m.? we ask. Yes, the man says. We came here as pilgrims to visit the shrine, we say, and all we have done so far is wait in line.

Where's the grace, God's gift of love to us? I guess it's the recognition of how impatient I am. I want things to happen *now*. Waiting forces us to give up the illusion that we are in control. That is a lesson I need to learn.

Part 5: Noise in the Night (Santiago de Compostella)

I am in Santiago de Compostella, in a remote part of western Spain. For hundreds of years, people have come to pray at the relics of the Apostle James, who is said to be buried behind the main altar. Many have walked here from around Europe and will stay at the hostels built for pilgrims in medieval times.

I am staying in a hotel. It has been a long journey here by train, and while I'm here I want to get a sense of this place pilgrims flock to for prayer and worship. The trouble is a rock band is playing loud music right across the street, and is showing no sign of stopping anytime soon. Even if I shut the patio doors and turn on the overhead fan, the sound radiates through my room. Given that the temperature today reached 38°C, I prefer to keep the doors open and the fan going. There is some relief with the breeze, despite the noise outside.

The challenge of being surrounded by noise – from the rock band, the vehicles moving up and down the street, people talking and laughing, or my self-induced busyness and psychic noise – is to find a quiet space deep within myself and be comfortable there. There are few places in the world where we can control the noise in and around us. Tom Stella, in his book *The God Instinct: Heeding Your Heart's Unrest*, writes about finding the place of solitude in our heart.[25] He quotes a story by Anthony DeMello:

> Said the Master to the businessman:
> "As the fish perishes on dry land, so you perish when you get entangled in the world. The fish must return to the water; you must return to solitude."
> The fisherman was aghast. "Must I give up my business and go into a monastery?"
> "No, no. Hold onto your business and go into your heart."[26]

In the same way, we can discover solitude in our hearts in the midst of the city noise. Wherever I am, my heart is, and that is where I will meet the Divine.

Part 6: Money Stolen (London)

When I arrived in London and opened my backpack to get my British money, it was gone! My Canadian money was gone, too. A lone U.S. $20 bill sat in the pouch. Everything else was still there: stacks of change from different countries and all my medications. Who did this? Why? How and where did it happen?

According to the literature on ancient pilgrimages, thieves were one of the biggest dangers along the way. Stories of pilgrims being robbed, sold into slavery or left for dead were not uncommon. Being robbed is a violation, and is hurtful, but the journey continues. In future, I will put my money into different parts of my backpack for safekeeping, but I will not be held hostage by fear. Instead, like my predecessors on the journey, I will keep trying to learn that I need to trust, remain vigilant, and be grateful for life and the path I follow.

Part 7: Pulling the Fragments Together (Midlife)

As I write this reflection, John McDermott sings a song on the radio about "when I grow too old to dream." I hope that by the time I grow too old to dream, I am either dead or suffering from dementia. While we always have choices about how we integrate spirituality and aging, our dreams help shape every part of our lives.

The Chinese philosopher Lao Tzu once wrote, "The journey of a thousand miles begins with a single step."

The journey into a living and meaningful spirituality demands that we take that first step. In midlife, we are forced to confront issues around meaning, purpose and vitality. We watch as friends move away, change or die. Children leave home. We wonder if we are doing the right thing with our lives. We may have accumulated social or professional status, money and friends, but we still hunger for something more. How we respond to that hunger groaning within us reveals a great deal about our openness to the push of the Spirit.

The single step Lao Tzu speaks of is an invitation to engage in the process. Listening to our hearts is the first step towards satisfying the hunger for renewed meaning and purpose. Many would agree with the opening lines of Dante's *Divine Comedy*: "In the middle of life's road/I found myself in a dark wood/the straight way ahead lost." Midlife is part of our journey. We can't control it or induce it. If we try to suppress it, we may lose our ability to dream, go deeper and enjoy life's many riches.

In midlife, we may feel less connected to the people, things and events around us. We may feel our sense of identity start to crumble. We may decide we need to experiment with our lives and evaluate where we have been and where we are going. For many, suppressed or repressed memories surface, and we must explore parts of our lives that we have forgotten. Health changes – for us or our friends or family members – reveal our frailty as humans. Death is no longer a remote concept; it is all too real. Like those who have walked before us, we realize that we have choices to make, dreams to fulfill. It's now or never.

As we face the choices that midlife thrusts upon us, we can try to cut the journey short, choose the wrong goal, run away or promise to deal with it tomorrow. We can spend more and more of our precious energy and time trying to avoid these inner stirrings by keeping busy, fleeing into distractions, or regressing to an earlier stage of our life. Whether we resist or surrender or do a little of both, the hunger for meaning and purpose gnawing within us will remain.

Along the way, the Spirit asks to be recognized. Even if we have been part of a faith community for many years, we may be crying out for something more. It's the desire for something more that can open us to the Spirit. Our search may require us to unlearn old patterns and walk in the darkness for a time.

Spirituality is about the glue that holds us together. During midlife, we need to define more deeply what spirituality means for us. Solitude allows us the opportunity and space to reconnect with the Divine. It invites us to sort through the stuff of our lives and shed those images, experiences, practices and values that no longer nurture us. Solitude also provides time for healing and focusing.

Another way to nourish our spirits is to be willing to suffer for and with another. I believe that genuine spirituality takes shape when we are willing to accompany another person through pain and suffering. In walking with another, we embrace a life of compassion and concern for ourselves, each other, society and all of creation.

Genuine spirituality also calls us to pay close attention to the restlessness within. Midlife is about shedding the old skin and allowing the more authentic me, the person God calls me to be, to emerge. It's about allowing ourselves to be converted anew by the circumstances that shape our lives.

What we start to realize during this period of transition is that God is finally getting our attention. In the past we may have been distracted by families, jobs and other responsibilities and pursuits. Now God is breaking through our defences and inviting us to a more authentic life. The Hasidim tell the story of a preacher who preached over and over: "Put God into your life; put God into your life!" But the holy rabbi of the village said, "Our task is not to put God into our lives. God is already there. Our task is simply to realize that."

Part 8: Getting down to Writing (Malta)

I find myself in Malta, a small island country in the Mediterranean Sea south of Italy. Why Malta? Like so many things that occur on a pilgrimage, pure chance led me to read an article on Malta in an in-flight magazine. From there, I went to the Internet, and now here I am. I hope to spend some time writing and pulling my thoughts about pilgrimage together.

I thought about staying in France in a rural village, Le Chambon, known for its commitment to providing

safe shelter to thousands of Jews during World War II.
After learning more about the village, however, I realized that its remoteness and its many tourist attractions
would not be conducive to writing.

Malta's surroundings reveal the country's ageless
rugged beauty. Before the nation was converted to
Christianity by the apostle Paul when he was shi-
pwrecked there in 60 AD, Malta was host to numerous
temples and religious traditions. While some of these
temples still exist, today Malta remains overwhelming
Catholic; most of the people attend church and participate in the religious festivals held throughout the
year. Catholic churches of all shapes and sizes as well
as convents of religious sisters are everywhere.

St. Paul's Shipwreck Church, for instance, contains
not only a relic of the apostle Paul but also part of the
pillar on which he was beheaded. It is located near
the co-cathedral of St. John, which was built by the
Knights of Malta as their main church between 1573
and 1578. Both churches are permeated by the history
and mystery of religious piety and experience. Their
incredible beauty is an example of how colour, design,
art and order can radiate something of the mystery of
God's presence.

The heart of Malta reveals the power of the Spirit
to draw people together, to mark important milestones
in life and give shape to their journey. The churches
are full. People pray together and light candles in front
of statues and pictures of Jesus, Mary and the saints.
For centuries, Christians there have gathered to pray,

celebrate their shared faith and engage in rituals that help bind the fragments of their lives into a meaningful pattern.

As I observe the faith of the people of Malta, I am reminded of the power of a religious experience that springs spontaneously from the depths of the soul. Captured in prayer, ritual and celebration, this type of experience nurtures the soul in good and bad times, providing hope amidst the darkness. It is a prayer that flows from the heart. In the lives of ordinary people, "the human spirit is the lamp of the Lord" (Proverbs 20:27).

Malta reminds me that the spiritual journey is about trusting in the abiding presence of God, in all things and in all people. While I came here to write and find out more about this place, I learned instead that God dwells among us in the simplest of ways. At the core of my religious experience I find the enduring mystery of a living God who strengthens, calls, prods, forgives and encourages me daily to become who I am called to be.

Reflection Questions

1. What outward experiences have given me the greatest opportunity to think more deeply about my life?

2. How have I experienced Saul Alinsky's comment in my own life: "Change means movement. Movement means friction"?

3. How do I discern the goodness or appropriateness of a given situation?

4. How have I encountered God in the surprising
    events of daily life?

Food for Thought

You are a child of God…
We were born to make manifest
the glory of God
that is within us.
It is not just in some of us;
it is in everyone.
And as we let our light shine,
we unconsciously give other people
permission to do the same.
As we are liberated from our own fear,
our presence automatically liberates others.
—Marianne Williamson

Epilogue

One Saturday morning, I was writing in my journal at my favourite coffee shop in Edmonton when a friend joined me. He asked, "What's up? How are you doing?" I hesitated and then said, "I feel out of sorts. I feel like a snake that sheds its skin every seven years: it's a time of transition. Something else is trying to take shape." He said, "That's not a comfortable feeling or an easy place to be." In acknowledging the uncertainty and anguish of the moment, he helped me to name what was happening.

"Shedding the skin" is a good analogy. I notice it at 4:00 a.m., when I wake up for a few minutes and have trouble getting back to sleep. I feel it in the way I am withdrawing from certain situations I have invested a great deal of time and effort in over the years. I feel it in my relationships, my work and my increasing comfort with my inner monk. The pilgrimage that began one sunny winter day in Lake Louise, Alberta, is coming to an end.

Since then, my life has changed dramatically. I am happier and more focused in terms of how I approach life, both internally and externally. I have a greater sense of mission, connection and purpose. I have come to love solitude more, and am more at home in my own skin. The journey has enabled me to be more myself, which has made life easier not only for me but also for others.

Yet the years have brought the usual mix of loss, surprises and joy. With my mother's death, I feel orphaned. Some friends have died, fallen ill or moved on in life's journey. Others have continued to nurture my life and challenge me. My dream of being a writer is taking shape: in 2003, I co-wrote with Ian Soles the book *Journey to Wholeness: Healing Body, Mind and Soul*. I also co-wrote an ethics book with Christopher Levan, *Knowing Your Ethical Preferences: A Working Guide*. And I have written articles that have been published in North America and Ireland.

I have changed jobs; some of my personal interests have sharpened and some have waned. I bought a second-hand piano in the hope of reviving my love of music. Instead, it has become the place where I display gifts, artifacts and reminders from my trips overseas. I gave up playing squash after I realized that if I don't play regularly, my body is more prone to injury and stress. The Holy Cross order continues to be my spiritual home and it keeps me focused on my calling. Yet, the order in North America continues to shrink and age rapidly; we are probably nearing the end of our time as a group on this continent. At the same time, I observe with joy the development and depth of my Holy Cross confreres in Asia, Africa, Haiti and South America.

Throughout all these movements and shifts has been the experience of a living God patiently walking with me. I am very aware of God's presence: sometimes

I welcome it, and at other times I flee it. No matter what happens, the God of Abraham and Sara, Jacob, Jeremiah, Joseph and Jesus stays with me – a gift in itself.

Today at Mass, the presider mentioned that he was setting off on a pilgrimage to Santiago de Compostella in Spain. He will begin at the French border and walk the entire month of June. I wish him well. I have visited Santiago, experienced the pilgrim's Mass with the mammoth censers filling the church with rich smells. Through the intensity of devotion, singing, incense and bells, pilgrims hear the voice of God calling them forth on their journey.

Where the next stage of my journey will lead, I do not know. But I do know from the journey I have just completed that I will continue to see God's presence in all things. I may not always recognize it, but I trust that God is walking with me.

On my journey so far, I have experienced sickness and good health, devastating poverty and rich landscapes, the overarching majesty of church, mosque, shrine and temple. I have prayed in rural chapels, reflected in ancient and new monasteries in North America and Europe, sat in awe in the great mosques of Turkey, and been moved by the religious fervour of pilgrims in Fatima, Montreal, Lourdes, Santiago de Compostella, Czestochowa and Auschwitz-Birkenau.

I hope to visit Iona, Chartres, Lourdes and the Isle of Lerins (St. Honoré) again. I know that if I am open, something new will emerge as I seek to shed the skin I have grown over the past few years and allow the new skin to emerge.

The words of the psalmist ultimately capture the essence of what I have learned so far on the pilgrim's journey:

> O Lord, you have searched me
> and known me.
> You know when I sit down
> and when I rise up;
> you discern my thoughts from far away.
> You search out my path and my lying down,
> and are acquainted with all my ways.
> (Psalm 139:1-3)

I can try to hide, set my own agenda, or hope to outwit fate, but ultimately, I need to hear and respond to God's call in my daily life. Like anyone, I stumble, but even when I stumble and become lost, I remember the love of a God who is passionate about my well-being and who guides me every step of the way.

Notes

1   Tom Stella, *The God Instinct: Heeding Your Heart's Unrest* (Notre Dame, IN: Sorin Books, 2001), 105.

2   *Praying Together in Word and Song*, 2nd rev. ed. (London: Mowbray, 1988), 30.

3   In *Thomas Merton, Spiritual Master: The Essential Writings*, Laurence Cunningham, ed. (Mahwah, NJ: Paulist Press, 1994), 431.

4   *Thomas Merton in Alaska: The Alaskan Conferences, Journals and Letters*, Robert Daggy, ed. (New York: New Directions, 1989), 112–13.

5   *The Intimate Merton: His Life from His Journals*, Patrick Hart and Jonathan Montaldo, eds. (San Francisco: HarperSanFrancisco, 1999), 164.

6   C.J. Jung, *Psychological Reflections: A New Anthology of His Writings*, Jolande Jacobi, ed. (New York: Bollingen Foundations, 1973), 316.

7   Jon Sobrino, "Spirituality and the Following of Jesus," in *Mysterium Liberationis: Fundamental Concepts of Liberation Theology* (Maryknoll, NY: Orbis, 1993), 677–701.

8   Herman Hesse, *Narcissus and Goldmund* (New York: Picador, 2003), 196.

9   Quoted in Phil Cousineau, *The Art of Pilgrimage: The Seeker's Guide to Making Travel Sacred* (Berkeley, CA: Conari Press), 126.

10 Jean Dalby Clift and Wallace B. Clift, *The Archetype of Pilgrimage: Outer Action with Inner Meaning* (New York: Paulist Press, 1996), 44.

11 Michael Kearney, MD, *Mortally Wounded: Stories of Soul Pain, Death and Healing* (New York: Touchstone, 1996), 63.

12 Carol Shields, *The Stone Diaries* (Toronto: Vintage Books, 1993), 297.

13 Casey, Michael, *The Undivided Heart: The Western Monastic Approach to Contemplation* (Petersham, MA: St. Bede's Publications, 1994), 36.

14 Casey, *The Undivided Heart*, 38, 39.

15 Casey, *The Undivided Heart*, 38.

16 *The Intimate Merton*, 127.

17 Quoted in Belden C. Lane, *The Solace of Fierce Landscapes: Exploring Desert and Mountain Spirituality* (New York: Oxford University Press, 1998), 24.

18 Edward Sellner, *Mentoring: The Ministry of Spiritual Kinship* (Notre Dame, IN: Ave Maria Press, 1990), 13.

19 Thomas Merton, *Seeds* (Boston: Shambhala, 2002), 63.

20 Quoted by Esther de Waal in *A Seven Day Journey with Thomas Merton* (Ann Arbor, MI: Servant Publications, 1992), 37–38.

21 "Worshipping Illusions: An Interview with Marion Woodman," in *Parabola*, Vol. XII, No. 2, May 1987, 59.

22 Quoted by Esther de Waal in *Lost in Wonder: Rediscovering the Spiritual Art of Attentiveness* (Ottawa: Novalis, 2003), 19.

23 Rainer Maria Rilke, *Letters to a Young Poet*, M.D. Herter, trans. (New York: W.W. Norton and Co., 1962), 35.

24 "The Throne of God" (Lecture given to the World Congress of Benedictine Abbots in Rome, September 2000), 100.

25 Stella, *The God Instinct*, 105.

26 Stella, *The God Instinct*, 13.

Further Reading

Albom, Mitch. *Tuesdays with Morrie*. New York: Doubleday, 1997.

Bell, Derrick. *Ethical Ambition: Living a Life of Meaning and Worth*. New York: Bloomsbury, 2002.

Bochen, Christine M., ed. *Thomas Merton's Essential Writings*. Maryknoll, NY: Orbis Books, 2003.

Bolen, Jean Shinoda. *Crossing to Avalon: A Woman's Midlife Journey*. New York: HarperSanFrancisco, 1993.

Bond, D. Stephenson. *The Archetype of Renewal: Psychological Reflections on the Aging, Death and Rebirth of the King*. Toronto: Inner City Books, 2003.

Bonhoeffer, Dietrich. *Life Together: A Discussion of Christian Fellowship*. New York: Harper & Row, 1976.

Burton-Christie, Douglas. The Word in the Desert: Scripture and the Quest for Holiness in Early Christian Monasticism. New York: Oxford University Press, 1993.

Campbell, Joseph. *Pathways to Bliss: Mythology and Personal Transformation*. Novato, CA: New World Library, 2004.

Carotenuto, Aldo. *Eros and Pathos: Shades of Love and Suffering*. Toronto: Inner City Books, 1989.

Casey, Michael. *The Undivided Heart: The Western Monastic Approach to Contemplation*. Petersham, MA: St. Bede's Publications, 1994.

Cowan, James. *Desert Father: A Journey in the Wilderness with Saint Anthony*. Boston: Shambhala, 2004.

Chittister, Joan D. *Called to Question: A Spiritual Memoir*. Lanham, MD: Sheed & Ward, 2004.

————. *Scarred by Struggle, Transformed by Hope*. Ottawa: Novalis, 2003.

Clift, Jean Dalby and Wallace B. Clift. *The Archetype of Pilgrimage: Outer Action with Inner Meaning*. New York: Paulist Press, 1996.

Coffin, William Sloan. *Credo*. Louisville, KY: Westminister John Knox Press, 2004.

Cousineau, Phil. *The Art of Pilgrimage: The Seeker's Guide to Making Travel Sacred*. Berkeley, CA: Conari Press. 1998.

Davis, Avram. *The Way of the Flame: A Guide to the Forgotten Mystical Tradition of Jewish Meditation*. New York: HarperSan-Francisco, 1996.

de Waal, Esther. *Lost in Wonder: Rediscovering the Spiritual Art of Attentiveness*. Ottawa: Novalis, 2003.

————. *Seeking God: The Way of St. Benedict*. Collegeville, MN: The Liturgical Press, 1984.

————. *A Seven Day Journey with Thomas Merton*. Ann Arbor, MI: Servant Publications, 1992.

Dieker, Bernadette and Jonathan Montaldo. *Merton & Hesychasm: The Prayer of the Heart…The Eastern Church*. Louisville, KY: Fons Vitae, 2003.

Dossey, Larry, MD. *Healing Words: The Power of Prayer and the Practice of Medicine*. New York: HarperSanFrancisco, 1993.

Egan, Keith, ed. *Carmelite Prayer: A Tradition for the 21ˢᵗ Century*. New York: Paulist Press, 2003.

Frankl, Victor. *Man's Search for Meaning*. New York: Washington Square Press, 1984.

Guggenbuhl-Craig, Adolf. *The Emptied Soul: On the Nature of Pathology*. Woodstock, CT: Spring Publications, 1980.

Gunn, Robert Jingen. *Journeys into Emptiness: Dogen, Merton, Jung and the Quest for Transformation*. New York: Paulist Press, 2000.

Hale, Robert. *Love on the Mountain: The Chronicle Journal of a Camaldolese Monk*. Trabuco Canyon, CA: Source Books and Hermitage Books, 1999.

Hammarskjold, Dag. *Markings*. Leif Sjoberg and W.H. Auden, trans. New York: Alfred A. Knopf, 1972.

Heschel, Abraham Joshua. *Moral Grandeur and Spiritual Audacity*. New York: The Noonday Press, 1996.

Hesse, Herman. *Narcissus and Goldmund*. New York: Picador, 1968.

Hillesum, Etty. *An Interrupted Life and Letters from Westerbork*. New York: An Owl Book, 1996.

Hillman, James. *The Force of Character and the Lasting Life*. New York: Random House, 1999.

―――. *The Soul's Code: In Search of Character and Calling*. New York: Random House, 1996.

Hollis, James. *Mythologems: Incarnations of the Invisible World*. Toronto: Inner City Books, 2004.

―――. *On This Journey We Call Our Life: Living the Questions*. Toronto: Inner City Books, 2003.

————. *Creating a Life: Finding Your Individual Path*. Toronto: Inner City Books, 2001.

————. *Swamplands of the Soul: New Life in Dismal Places*. Toronto: Inner City Books, 1996.

————. *Tracking the Gods: The Place of Myth in Modern Life*. Toronto: Inner City Books, 1995.

————. *Under Saturn's Shadow: The Wounding and Healing of Men*. Toronto: Inner City Books, 1994.

Inchausti, Robert. *Thomas Merton's American Prophecy*. Albany, NY: State University of New York, 1998.

Jaffe, Lawrence W. *Liberating the Heart: Spirituality and Jungian Psychology*. Toronto: Inner City Books, 1990.

Johnson, Robert A. *The Fisher King & The Handless Maiden*. New York: HarperSanFrancisco, 1993.

Johnson, Robert A. and Jerry M. Ruhl. *Contentment: A Way to True Happiness*. New York: HarperCollins, 1999.

Jones, Alan. *The Soul's Journey: Exploring the Three Passages of the Spiritual Life with Dante as a Guide*. New York: HarperCollins, 1995.

Kearney, Michael. *A Place of Healing: Working with Suffering in Living and Dying*. Oxford: Oxford University Press, 2000.

————. *Mortally Wounded: Stories of Soul Pain, Death and Healing*. New York: Touchstone, 1996.

Kreinheder, Albert. *Body and Soul: The Other Side of Illness*. Toronto: Inner City Books, 1991.

Kushner, Harold S. *Living a Life that Matters: Resolving the Conflict Between Conscience and Success*. New York: Alfred A. Knopf, 2001.

Louf, André. *The Cistercian Way*. Kalamazoo, MI: Cistercian Publications, 1989.

Luke, Helen. *Such Stuff as Dreams Are Made On: The Autobiography and Journals of Helen M. Luke*. New York: Parabola Books, 2000.

Maddix, Thomas D. and Ian C. Soles. *Journey to Wholeness: Healing Body, Mind and Soul*. Ottawa: Novalis, 2003.

Merton, Thomas. *Seeds*. Boston: Shambhala, 2002.

———. *Thomas Merton in Alaska: The Alaskan Conference, Journals and Letters*. New York: A New Directions Book, 1988.

Merton, Thomas and Jean Leclercq. *Survival or Prophecy? The Letters of Thomas Merton and Jean Leclercq*. New York: Farrar, Straus and Giroux, 2002.

Moyers, Bill. *Healing and the Mind*. New York: Doubleday, 1993.

Niebuhr, H. Richard. *The Responsible Self: An Essay in Christian Moral Philosophy*. New York: Harper & Row, 1978.

Norris, Kathleen. *The Cloister Walk*. New York: Riverhead Books, 1996.

———. *Dakota: A Spiritual Geography*. Boston: Houghton Mifflin, 1993.

Nouwen, Henri. *The Inner Voice of Love*. New York: Doubleday, 1996.

O'Donohue, John. *Anam Cara: A Book of Celtic Wisdom*. New York: Cliff Street Books, 1997.

Palmer, Helen. *The Enneagram in Love and Work: Understanding Your Intimate & Business Relationships*. New York: Harper Collins, 1995.

Pannikar, Raimundo. *Blessed Simplicity: The Monk as Universal Archetype*. New York: Seabury Press, 1988.

Parker, Palmer, J. *Let Your Life Speak: Listening for the Voice of Vocation*. San Francisco: Jossey-Bass, 2000.

Rilke, Rainer Maria.M.D. *Letters to a Young Poet*. Herter Norton, trans. New York: W.W. Norton, 1962.

Rohr, Richard and Andreas Ebert. *The Enneagram: A Christian Perspective*. New York: Crossroad, 2004.

Savin, Olga, trans. *The Way of the Pilgrim*. Boston: Shambhala, 1996.

Sellner, Edward. *Mentoring: The Ministry of Spiritual Kinship*. Notre Dame, IN: Ave Maria Press, 1990.

Spohn, William C. *Go and Do Likewise: Jesus and Ethics*, New York: Continuum, 2000.

Taylor, John V. *A Matter of Life and Death*. London: SCM Press, 1986.

Thompson, C. Michael. *The Congruent Life: Following the Inward Path to Fulfilling Work and Inspired Leadership*. San Francisco: Jossey-Bass Publishers, 2000.

Toibin, Colm. *The Sign of the Cross: Travels in Catholic Europe*. London: Jonathan Cape, 1994.

Walsh, John, O.Carm. *The Carmelite Way: An Ancient Path for Today's Pilgrim*. New York: Paulist Press, 1996.

Whyte, David. *The Heart Aroused: Poetry and the Preservation of the Soul in Corporate America*. New York: Doubleday, 1994.

Wright, Wendy M. *Sacred Heart: Gateway to God*. London: Darton, Longman and Todd, 2002.

Journey to Wholeness
Healing body, mind and soul

THOMAS D. MADDIX and IAN C. SOLES

The journey through life is filled with highs and lows, successes and failures, hurt and hope. Each of us longs to be whole – physically, spiritually, emotionally, psychologically. At the same time, fear may hold us back from finding meaning and wholeness in our lives. How can we find our way?

Journey to Wholeness is a fascinating exploration of physical and spiritual healing written by two experts: counsellor Tom Maddix and massage therapist Ian Soles. Through a series of reflections on spirituality, stories of people who have sought massage therapy, and insights about people in search of answers to big questions, this inspiring book examines the interconnectedness of mind, body and soul and offers a road map for how to get there.

Available from Novalis
1-800-387-7164
www.novalis.ca